HOW TO MAKE

MOVING
WOODEN TOYS

HOW TO MAKE
MOVING WOODEN TOYS

Peter Holland

CASSELL

A CASSELL BOOK
First published 1995
by Cassell
Villiers House
41/47 Strand
London
WC2N 5JE

Copyright © Peter Holland 1995

Designed by Andrew Schoolbred
Photography by Paul Bricknell

Distributed in the United States
by Sterling Publishing Co., Inc.
387 Park Avenue South, New York, New York 10016-8810

Distributed in Australia
by Capricorn Link (Australia) Pty Ltd
2/13 Carrington Road
Castle Hill
NSW 2154

British Library Cataloguing-in-Publication Data
A catalogue record for this book is available from the
British Library

ISBN 0-304-34368-4
Typeset by Litho Link Ltd, Welshpool, Powys, Wales
Printed and bound in Slovenia

CONTENTS

INTRODUCTION

Making wooden toys is a tradition going back many thousands of years; a craft practised by many people for their children, long before such things became a saleable commodity. Often figurines, dolls were whittled with a small knife from odd pieces of kindling wood, later to be equipped with movable joints, formed by integral hinges and pivoted on thin pegs. There is a wealth of inspiration in some of the very early Russian and Polish examples, but the use of more mechanical mechanisms has widened the scope of the most simple toy.

This is not to say that this book is all about mechanical models, whose ideal place is in a display cabinet, and which demand the use of an elaborate workshop and the skill of a woodcarver. No, if you want to make some of the 20 projects in this book to give to a young relative, you will find the projects' full-size template pages and step-by-step instructions will guide you through the exercise. In doing this, you will not only provide something different, something upon which you have used care and love, but something that will be a constant reminder that there are things that are special, worth more than money spent on plastic playthings.

These toys are interactive; they invite the user to experiment rather than be entertained, and to see that the world of making things is open to anyone who is willing to spend a little time.

The tools are few and simple; the rest you will pick up as you turn these pages and have a little 'hands-on' practice. There are plenty of helpful tips dotted among the projects and anything remotely technical is at the end, so as not to get in the way of those of you who have already used a fretsaw, drill, screwdriver and chisel. Just pitch in and enjoy; you will be getting the first crack at having fun while you make the projects. Each toy has been specially designed so that there are no loose pieces which might be swallowed, or sharp edges. The brightly coloured paint, which make these toys so attractive, is non-toxic. The age of the recipient will control the choice of subject but, in some cases, it is possible to scale down the handle length of the larger examples, to suit their height.

WHERE TO WORK

The toys described in this set of projects can be made in quite a small space. If you have a garden shed or corner of the garage, it will be more than large enough for both storing the small amount of wood and leaving enough space around a small workbench or Workmate type of portable bench. The dimensions in Fig. 1 will give you some idea of the area you and the job in hand will occupy with comfort.

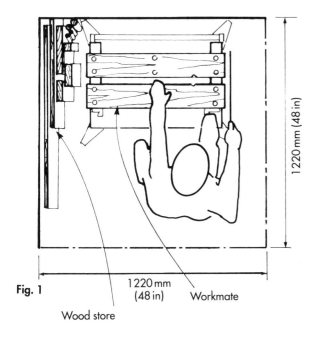

Fig. 1

1220 mm (48 in)

1220 mm (48 in)

Workmate

Wood store

Storage
The toys are small in terms of general woodwork subjects, so most of the space will be needed for cutting larger pieces of wood down to the sizes that will be given in the materials list in each project. Much will depend on what wood you already have, how many of the projects immediately take your eye, and what sizes you purchase from your local wood-yard or DIY shop.

In the latter case, you will find that wood comes in standard lengths and panel sizes, but you may find that a friendly wood-yard will cut to exactly the sizes you need from odd short-ends left by someone's earlier order. They charge to the nearest metre or yard, so it will pay you to combine several projects in one buying session. You can then cut the wood to the most convenient lengths for storage in the shed or garage.

Bear in mind, however, that the lengths shown in the materials lists are minimum. If you cut for convenience only, you may find that one project is short! The amount of space for storage is quite small, so do not worry about separating the wood into individual projects.

Cutting
You will also find that it is convenient to cut parts out from the wood stock of several projects, rather than separating the individual quantities. Then there is usually an area of wood to clamp down before you reach the bitter end. There is a separate chapter dealing with your choice of materials, so now consider the working area.

Bench space
In addition to the bench, fixed or portable (like a Workmate), you need a small table or cabinet on which to place either a drill stand for an electric drill, or a power fretsaw (sometimes known as a scroll saw); one item at a time, if space is at a premium. The area for this and yourself is shown in Fig. 2.

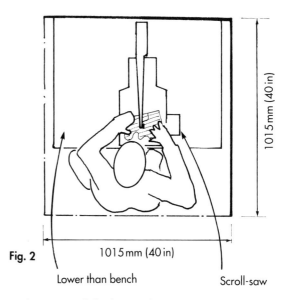

Fig. 2

1015 mm (40 in)

1015 mm (40 in)

Lower than bench

Scroll-saw

As some of the larger fretsaws are heavy, it is best to allocate one space for this item, then use the main

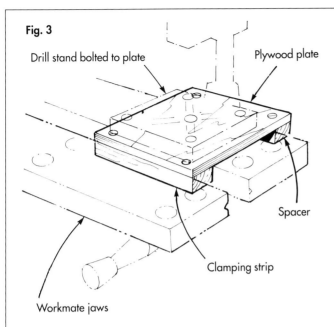

Fig. 3

Drill stand bolted to plate

Plywood plate

Spacer

Clamping strip

Workmate jaws

bench or Workmate as a temporary mount for the drill stand. The best stability in the latter case is to have a block of wood under a thick plywood panel on which the drill stand is mounted. You can then clamp the base in the jaws, as shown in Fig. 3. The drill stand will also stand level when placed on a table or bench, due to the second strip of wood underneath, which should be spaced just to clear the width of one of the Workmate jaws (Fig. 4).

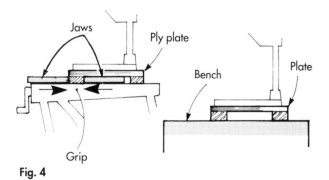

Jaws

Ply plate

Bench

Plate

Grip

Fig. 4

Sanding

One power tool that I would consider important is the belt sander. It removes wood and smoothes it accurately and fast. With a fine grit belt, it is better than an orbital sander, which many households have. Small toy parts just vibrate under this, whereas the belt job strokes them smooth in one direction, while it can sit in its own bench clamp, on the main or portable bench.

In for a jig?

Popular in some households is the power jigsaw. This hand-held tool will cut smooth, but not very sharp, curves in thin or thick wood. However, the small parts in these toys are difficult to hold, either by themselves, or in a small piece of wood, as you get near the end of it.

If you are buying, I suggest that you choose a power fretsaw in this case. If you already have one, there is a use for it in one of the tips on making wheels.

By hand

If you only have a hand-frame fretsaw, the fretwork jobs will take rather longer, but then time spent is pleasure time. Be comfortable, however: have a low stool so that if you mount a fretsaw cutting clamp on the Workmate, you are at a suitable height to work (Fig. 5).

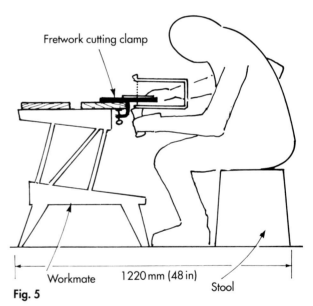

Fretwork cutting clamp

Workmate

1220 mm (48 in)

Stool

Fig. 5

Overlapping

When you come to the painting stages of the projects, it is convenient to have a wide shelf or loose panel of plywood or hardwood, which you can lay over the bench area (as in Fig. 6) to form a storage and drying area while you get on with the painting. Naturally, you will not be doing any woodwork that raises dust at this stage, so it is something to programme during the evening, when neighbours or the household want to be quiet.

An ideal workspace is shown in Fig. 7, but it can be re-shaped to suit the end of the garage, or even in

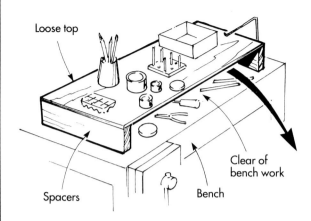

Loose top

Clear of
bench work

Spacers

Bench

Fig. 6

part of a utility room in the house. The best thing
about toy making is the small area that the actual
work area takes up, and even though I have the
facilities of a shed workshop that is 2 by 2.7 m
(about 6½ by 9 ft), other work was going on in the
same period of time.

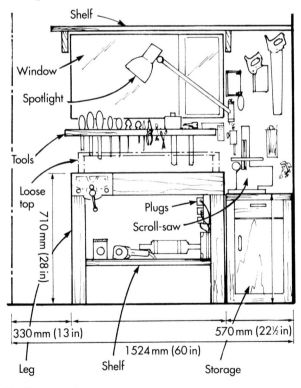

Shelf

Window

Spotlight

Tools

Loose
top

710 mm (28 in)

Plugs

Scroll-saw

330 mm (13 in)   570 mm (22½ in)

1524 mm (60 in)

Leg   Shelf   Storage

Fig. 7

Tips

- Arrange plenty of natural light and a good
  adjustable spotlight for evening work. Poor
  lighting leads to spoilt work and accidents.

- Keep it dry. The wood will not be in the best
  condition if it is taken from a warm, dry DIY shop
  or under cover in a wood-yard, then put in a cold,
  damp garage or potting-shed. As you work it, it
  will be drying out, then it will shrink or warp
  when it gets into a household environment. Toys
  that have wood-to-wood moving parts will seize
  up with this type of ill treatment.

- Keep the dust at bay. Not only is wood dust
  harmful to your lungs, but if it is still hanging
  about in the air or on supposedly clean surfaces, it
  can ruin the paint job. If the floor of the work area
  is concrete, this is a dusty area too. Use a floor
  paint to reduce the unwanted addition to sawdust.
  Do not forget that even if you have a breathing
  pad or mask for the woodworking jobs, you may
  forget to wear it for the sweeping up afterwards.
  Such energetic action promotes hard breathing, as
  well as transferring dust to areas that you thought
  you had dusted. Your scroll saw has a dust blower
  to clear the cutting area, but not all have dust
  collectors. The belt or orbital sander should have a
  dust collecting bag, but this does not remove all
  the fine dust that flies off the job.

  A cylinder-type vacuum cleaner should also be
  part of the workshop equipment, even if on loan
  from the household. Just because the toys do not
  involve a lot of woodwork, it does not mean that
  these little details do not matter. One spoilt paint
  job is enough to remind you to keep the work area
  clean and tidy.

SKATER

Although this is a simple spinning toy, it demonstrates dynamics, in that you can now see why skaters can increase the speed of their spins without using their feet. They start a spin with arms spread out, then draw them in. Fig. 1 shows what happens. The weight of the arms, represented by spots on the circle, are moving at a given speed. At a large radius (A), this speed will take them, say, one quarter of a turn. But if the radius is reduced at this time (B), the speed will not have dropped much, so the same distance will occupy half a turn. In other words, the revolutions per minute will double. Of course, you get nothing for free, and with nowhere else to put the arms, the speed will gradually drop.

Right! This toy has weights in the arms (Fig. 2) and the arms are pulled in by a piece of thread coming out at the feet. Your youngster can use it to learn about dynamics. Just show him or her the easy two-part play technique (see Fig. 3). Hold the top thread and flip the feet round between the other finger and thumb, to make it spin. The arms will open out . . . Now to Fig. 4. While the toy is spinning, gently pull the bottom thread to bring the arms inwards, and the figure will speed up.

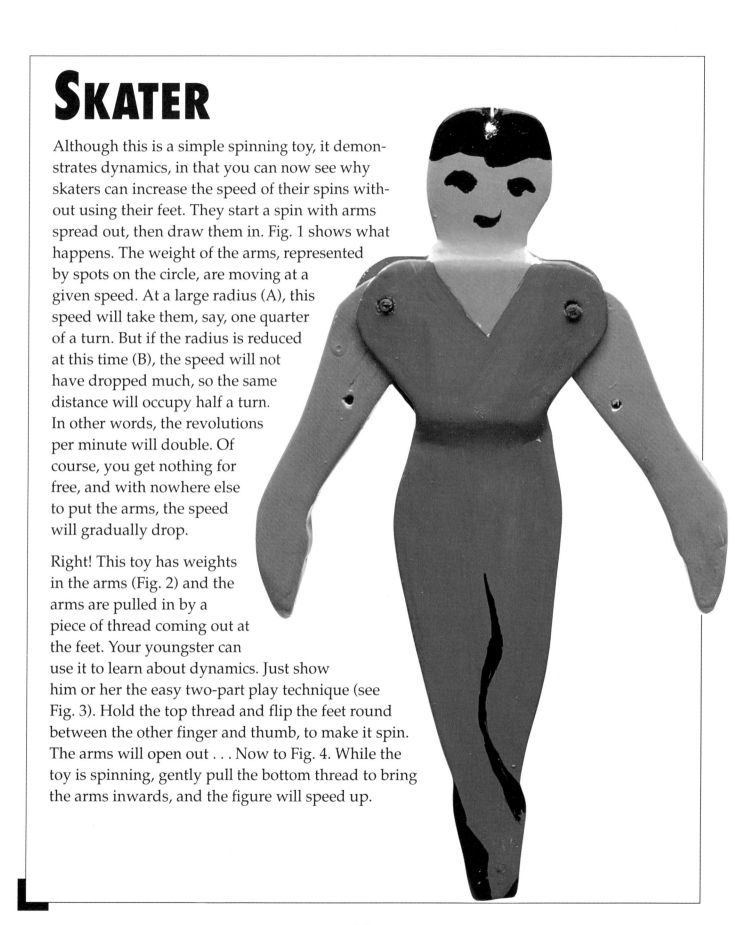

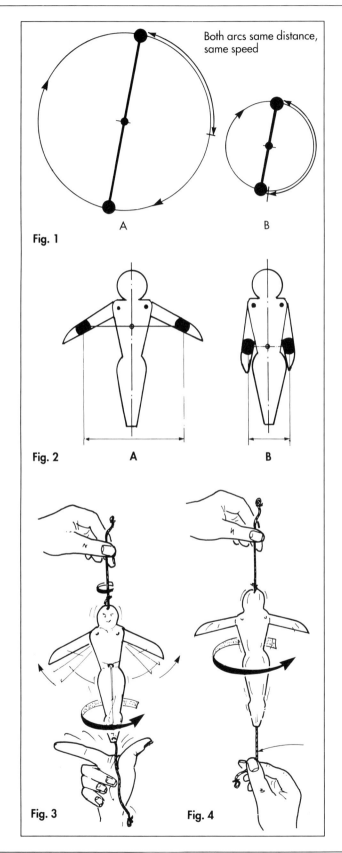

Fig. 1

Both arcs same distance, same speed

A   B

Fig. 2   A   B

Fig. 3   Fig. 4

MATERIALS

1 mm (1/32 in) plywood or
    Formica: 10 x 64 mm
    (2½ x 4 in)
9 mm (3/8 in) plywood:
    175 x 51 mm (7 x 2 in)
Two small staples
Panel-pins
Short piece of 2 mm (3/32 in) dowel
    or plastic cotton-bud stick
Carpet thread
Plumber's solder (for weight)
PVA glue
Paint

TOOLS

Fretsaw
Drill
Hammer
Soldering-iron
Sandpaper
Paintbrushes
Pencil
Carbon paper
Rule
Scissors

1 Start with the arms. Cut two rectangular blanks of the thick plywood, large enough to accept the outline of the arm template on page 13. You only need trace the arm on to one piece. Temporarily fix the blanks together with three panel-pins, one of which goes through the cross marking the shoulder pivot hole. The pins must not stick out underneath, or they will prevent the blanks lying flat or sliding on the sawing table. You can use a hand or power fretsaw or scroll-saw. The latter type will cut a true vertical line. If you hand saw, with the blade not upright, one of the arms will not match the other . . . Wait a moment, though. The first thing to do is to make the holes in the arms that are to take the weights.

2 Study Fig. 5. Drill within the centre outline so that you can thread in the saw blade, and fret out to the line. Do not cut the outer edge yet, because it will be easier to fill the hole with melted solder, while there is plenty of wood around it.

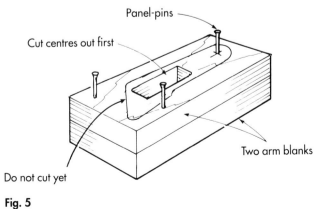

Panel-pins

Cut centres out first

Do not cut yet

Two arm blanks

Fig. 5

3 Now to Fig. 6. Gently prise the two pieces of wood apart and fix each in turn to a scrap of thicker wood, using the same panel-pins in the same holes. You can now use the soldering-iron to melt solder into the holes you have just cut. Fill right flush; fill off any excess above and below.

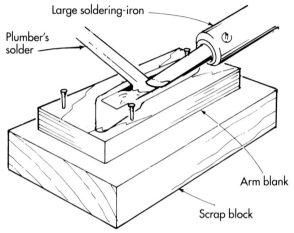

Large soldering-iron

Plumber's solder

Arm blank

Scrap block

Fig. 6

4 Pin them together as before, fret all round (Fig. 7), then remove the pins and drill as indicated. Sand and fill the grain. You can use car body filler if the solder is still not smooth. You might find a couple of pieces of brass or steel of the right size to use instead of solder, but they have to be equal in weight and heavy enough. Fix these with fast epoxy and fill flush as above.

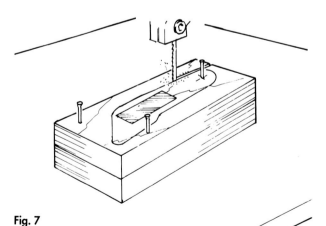

Fig. 7

5 Return to the patterns. Mark out the shoulder and spacer shapes on the thin plywood or Formica. Cut the shoulders as a pair, by taping a couple of rectangles together. Drill as one also. Mark out and cut the body in the thick plywood. Align the sholders via the holes, and glue them to the body (see Fig. 8).

Fig. 8

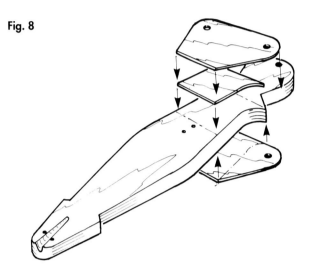

6 Sand, fill and paint the body and arms. When dry, tap in the two staples and hinge the arms in place with dowels or cotton-bud sticks, as in Fig. 9. They must move very freely. It is better to enlarge the holes in the arms and have the holes in the thin plywood shoulders tight. This gives a longer working life, because there is more bearing area. When in place, put a spot of glue on each end of the dowels to fix them to the shoulders.

Fig. 9

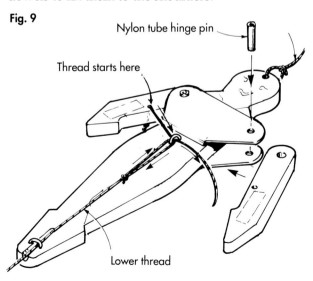

Nylon tube hinge pin

Thread starts here

Lower thread

7 Tie carpet thread to the head via the hole there – 100 mm (4 in) is enough. With the arms extended fully, knot a second piece and thread it through the arm, through the top staple, make a loop and back through the staple from the same side, then through the other arm, and knot it. Tie a third piece of thread at the centre of the loop and adjust it so that when it passes through the bottom staple, the arms move equally. There should be about 100 mm (4 in) of thread below the feet. When the thread becomes bunched up with much twisting in use, spin the toy in the opposite direction to untangle it.

TIP

Cutting thin laminate

Some parts of the toys are made from very thin plywood, which you can buy from model shops – it is used for model aeroplanes and boats. If you do not have a model shop close by, you may use plastic laminate, such as Formica or even thinner, kitchen surfacing laminates, obtainable from the offcuts bin at hardware or DIY shops.

This laminate is hard and needs to be cut with a very fine fretsaw blade after parting a suitable area from the scrap piece with a hacksaw or hacksaw blade in a pad-saw handle. Shaped pieces need to be taped down firmly to a sacrificial piece of plywood, say, 3 mm (⅛ in) thick. This prevents the blade stroke becoming jerky and splintering the cut edge of the thin material (see the diagram). You can cut the thinness of plywood singly, alone, with old scissors, but that thicker plywood taped underneath enables you to make intricate fretsaw cuts.

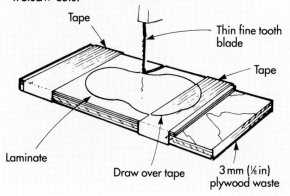

Tape

Thin fine tooth blade

Tape

Laminate

Draw over tape

3 mm (⅛ in) plywood waste

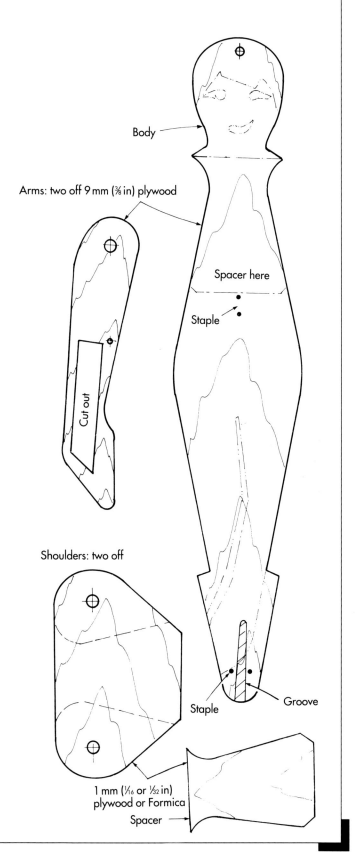

Body

Arms: two off 9 mm (⅜ in) plywood

Spacer here

Staple

Cut out

Shoulders: two off

Staple

Groove

1 mm (¹⁄₁₆ or ¹⁄₃₂ in) plywood or Formica

Spacer

13

BOXERS

The traditional Russian parallelogram stick toys take several forms. This project is adapted from a side-by-side version in which the figures swivel in upright positions (Fig. 1). As the boxer from the red corner swings with his right, the one from the blue corner dodges left, and gets hit on the nose. Then as the sticks are moved (as in Fig. 2), he swings with his left and clashes gloves. Although both figures have the same basic component, the arms of one are angled up a little so that they can clear each other for the nose blow! It's a toy to take away your anger.

Fig. 1

Fig. 2

MATERIALS

9 mm (⅜ in) plywood:
 177 x 152 mm (7 x 6 in)
19 x 6 mm (¾ x ¼ in) pine:
 580 mm (23 in)
Four No. 10 16 mm (⅝ in)
 countersunk woodscrews
PVA glue
Paint

TOOLS

Fretsaw
Drill
Countersink
Screwdriver
Sandpaper
Paintbrushes
Pencil
Carbon paper
Rule

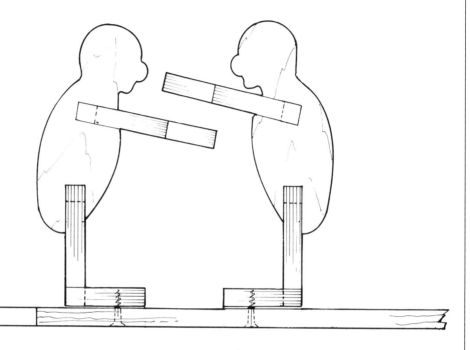

Fig. 3

1 Using carbon paper and a hard pencil, trace down the template shapes on page 17 on to the plywood. If you plan the position of these shapes, you can cut pairs by fixing two rectangles together with panel-pins, as you did for the Skater, and so reducing the cutting time. Do not make the notch to receive the arms in the body while pair cutting. This is why the two bodies are drawn separately in the patterns.

2 Sand all the edges and try the notches for fit between the components. The joint between each leg and foot needs to be a snug fit. No sloppiness here, please; there is quite a load on the ankles when the fight is on. Sand all the surfaces that are to be painted before assembly, because it is much easier to do this when they are flat on the bench.

3 Glue the legs to the bodies first; the notches interlock fully, so that the lower end of the body meets the crotch at the rear face. Remember to turn one pair of arms over so that the longer arm of each boxer is on the same side of the toy (Fig. 3). Then, following Fig. 4, set the tilt of the arms and check that when glued, the feet are at 90 degrees to the legs (Fig. 5). They must be left and right types if you have cut them asymmetrically. Mark all the hole positions on their sole surface.

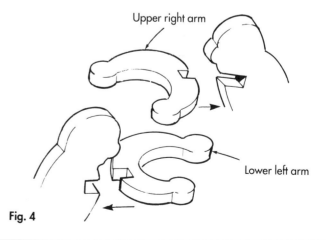

Upper right arm

Lower left arm

Fig. 4

4 Cut the pine strip in half and round off the ends to form the pair of sticks. Drill and countersink where shown on the templates. Sand and paint them, and check that screws will turn easily in their holes (the paint may have clogged them). Had you painted first, there might be a risk of marking the finish, should the drill raise a splinter as it exits.

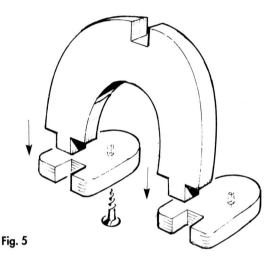

Fig. 5

5 After the paint has set on the boxers, pierce the hole positions just deep enough to start a woodscrew. Assemble the sticks to the boxers with the screws only just biting. Gently test to see if the action is correct, then remove the screws. If the gloves do not contact where intended, re-position the offending hole. Only then, drill the pilot holes in the feet, from the soles up, using a piece of masking tape in the drill bit. This will serve as a depth gauge and prevent the hole coming right through. You can now finish and paint the boxers in opposing colours.

6 When the paint has hardened, screw the sticks to the feet, as shown in Fig. 1. Do not tighten them; leave enough freedom for easy movement. The screws should still be stiff to turn, so that inquisitive users cannot take it apart. Crosshead screws are best, as there are no sharp corners. Should you have drilled the pilot holes too large, and find a screw too easy to undo, take it out and put a tiny spot of fast epoxy glue on its tip, before replacing it.

TIP

Small right-angle clamp

Where a tiny joint needs to be clamped at right angles, as in the feet of the Boxers project, the method shown in the diagram may help. You need a small piece of alloy angle section from a DIY shop, a short piece of square section wood and two, strong, short rubber bands.

Rest the glued-up joint in the hollow of the angle strip, lay the wood section in the joint angle and apply the bands tightly. Wind each band over one turn at a time to balance the pressure, otherwise the wood strip will tilt.

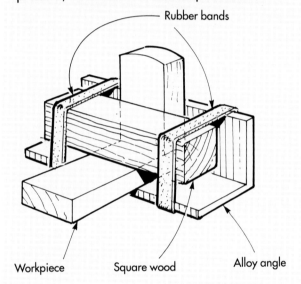

Rubber bands

Workpiece   Square wood   Alloy angle

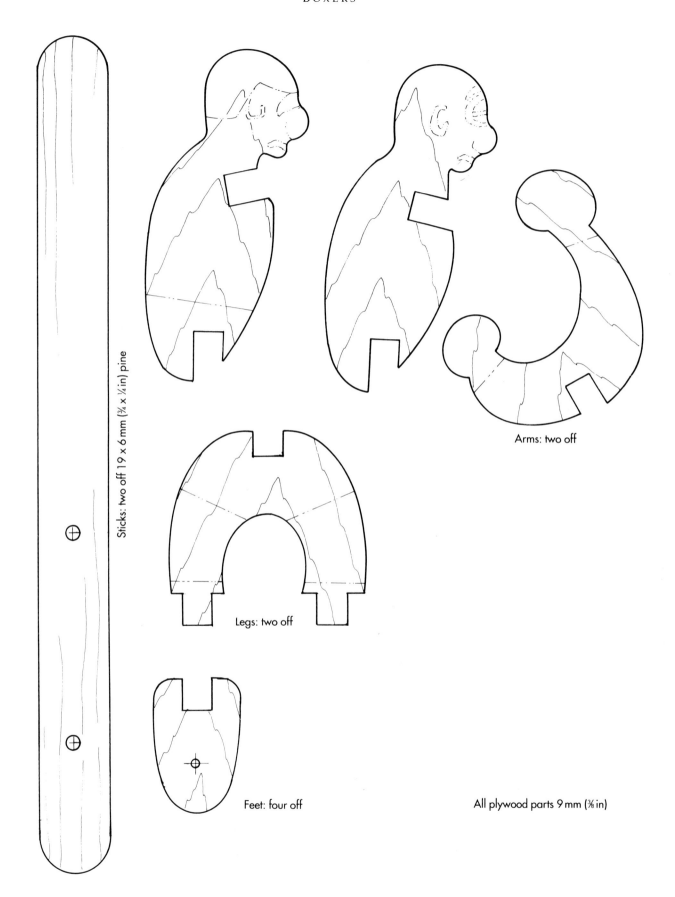

Sticks: two off 19 x 6mm (¾ x ¼in) pine

Arms: two off

Legs: two off

Feet: four off

All plywood parts 9mm (⅜in)

SWING WING

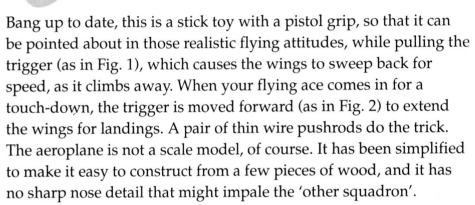

Bang up to date, this is a stick toy with a pistol grip, so that it can be pointed about in those realistic flying attitudes, while pulling the trigger (as in Fig. 1), which causes the wings to sweep back for speed, as it climbs away. When your flying ace comes in for a touch-down, the trigger is moved forward (as in Fig. 2) to extend the wings for landings. A pair of thin wire pushrods do the trick. The aeroplane is not a scale model, of course. It has been simplified to make it easy to construct from a few pieces of wood, and it has no sharp nose detail that might impale the 'other squadron'.

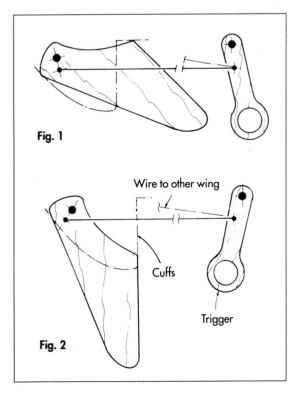

Fig. 1

Wire to other wing

Cuffs

Trigger

Fig. 2

MATERIALS
3 mm (⅛ in) plywood:
   228 x 202 mm (9 x 8 in)
9 mm plywood (⅜ in):
   114 x 64 mm (4½ x 2½ in)
19 mm (¾ in) pine:
   241 x 42 mm (9½ x 1⅝ in)
3 mm (⅛ in) dowel: 25 mm (1 in)
9 mm (⅜ in) dowel: 241 mm
   (9½ in)
Springy 1 mm steel wire
   (18 swg): 660 mm (26 in)
One No. 6 12 mm (½ in)
   woodscrew
PVA glue
Paint

TOOLS
Fretsaw
Coping saw
   (optional)
Drill
Screwdriver
Hammer
Snipe-nose pliers
Chisel
Rat-tail file
Sandpaper
Pencil
Carbon paper
Rule
Paintbrushes

1 Trace off the 3 mm shapes from the template on page 21 and fret out the wings as a pair and the cuffs as a stack of four – all temporarily fixed together with panel-pins, preferably in the waste area; although one pin through any of the hole positions will ensure accurate alignment later on. Note how this multiple-cutting technique speeds things up and ensures matching pieces. Do remember, however, not to allow the panel-pin points to project through the underside of the stack. They will drag on the saw table, then let go with a jerk, spoiling the smooth line or breaking the blade.

2 Transfer the fuselage pattern shape to the side of the pine strip and saw it out. You can use a coping saw if the fretsaw is not up to it, although power fretsaws can usually cope well. Do not be tempted to use a coarse-bladed power jigsaw. These hand-held machines are a little too fierce for handling small pieces of work, unless, that is, they have a bench mount that is designed for them. All the prototype toys were made with a scroll-saw.

3 Remove the wood from the wing position by drilling and cleaning up with a chisel until three scrap pieces of 3 mm (⅛ in) ply fit loosely inside. This will allow the wings to swing easily between the other ply pieces (known as 'cuffs'). The side and scrap top view are shown in Fig. 3. Note that the lugs or tenons on the cuffs have to fit into the slot you have made.

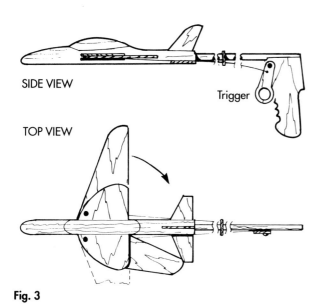

SIDE VIEW

Trigger

TOP VIEW

Fig. 3

4 Whittle down a waste piece of the 19 mm (¾ in) pine to form a spacer that will hold the cuffs against the fuselage hole (mortise). There should be enough clearance to accommodate a piece of the wire without friction, when the wing panel is inserted over it. This detail is shown in Fig. 4. Having tried all this dry, take a chisel and sandpaper to the edges of the fuselage outline where indicated, and round it off to form a cockpit and nicely shaped nose. If you shape these areas before getting the wing mounting slot right, the fuselage will be difficult to clamp in the vice.

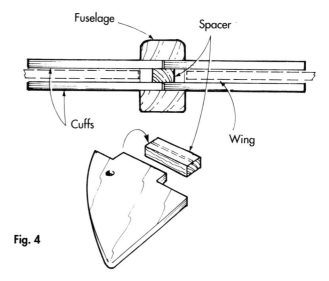

Fuselage

Spacer

Cuffs

Wing

Fig. 4

5 Drill the tail end to take the 9 mm (⅜ in) dowel rod before you carve a V groove to take the fin, which also needs to be chamfered on both sides (Fig. 5). If the groove is made before you have drilled, there will be a risk of the wood splitting. Just to be on the safe side, you could glue in the dowel and tackle the groove when it has set.

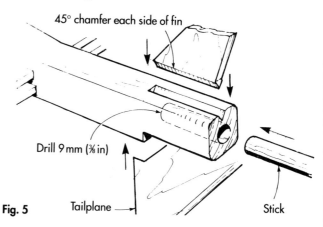

45° chamfer each side of fin

Drill 9 mm (⅜ in)

Tailplane

Stick

Fig. 5

6 You can now sand the model components and glue them to the fuselage. Push a piece of 3 mm (⅛ in) dowel through the cuffs and wing panels before the glue sets to check that they are aligned correctly. Do not glue the dowel yet.

7 Transfer the pattern shape to the 9 mm (⅜ in) plywood. This is the pistol grip. Initially with a saw, then with a rat-tail file and, finally, with sandpaper wrapped around the dowel, form a groove in the top edge to take the latter. Drill a pilot hole for the woodscrew on the left-hand side, where shown. The smallest piece of wood is the 3 mm (⅛ in) plywood wire guide. Drill before cutting – it is easier to hold, and there is less chance of it splitting. Slide it on to the dowel, small holes down, and glue it half-way along. Glue the dowel into the groove in the plywood grip.

8 Remove the wings to finish and paint the whole toy.

9 Now for the wire; two equal lengths, please. The prototype uses springy wires from an old magazine binder. Bend the last 3 mm (⅛ in) of each to a sharp 90-degree angle. To get it really sharp, put the short end in the metal vice and hammer the bend down square. It should fit the small hole in each wing without protruding out the other side (see Fig. 6). Test with the wire and wing in place on its 3 mm (⅛ in) pivot dowel.

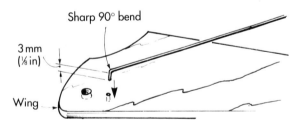

Fig. 6

10 Make the trigger from 3 mm (⅛ in) plywood, and mount it on its pivot screw in the grip. Thread both wires through the small holes in the guide, with the bent ends forward. Insert these ends into the wings from below and put the wings back on their dowel pivots. The rear ends will be shaped next. Fig. 7 shows the general shape, but before the grip is fixed. The exact length can be determined by measuring each with the wire bent at right angles in line with the hole in the trigger. The wing should be swept back fully when the trigger is back against the grip. A small finger through the hole will indicate this position. The idea is to adjust the wires until both wings move the same amount.

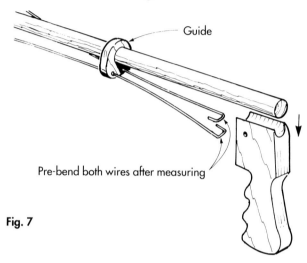

Fig. 7

11 Remove the trigger and thread the now accurately bent wires through the same small hole. Follow the sequence in Fig. 8. Twist the trigger to follow the bends in first one wire, then the other. It should look like C. Screw the trigger back but allow it to move freely. If the screw can be loosened easily, put a spot of fast epoxy glue on the tip and replace it. It is important to ensure that smaller children do not get hold of tiny parts which large children may have forcibly removed. The best answer for unscrewed screws is to fill the crosshead recess with fast epoxy, after the screw is set in place firmly, and then to smooth it off.

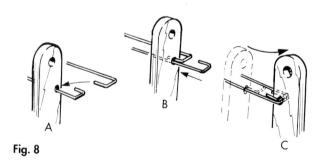

Fig. 8

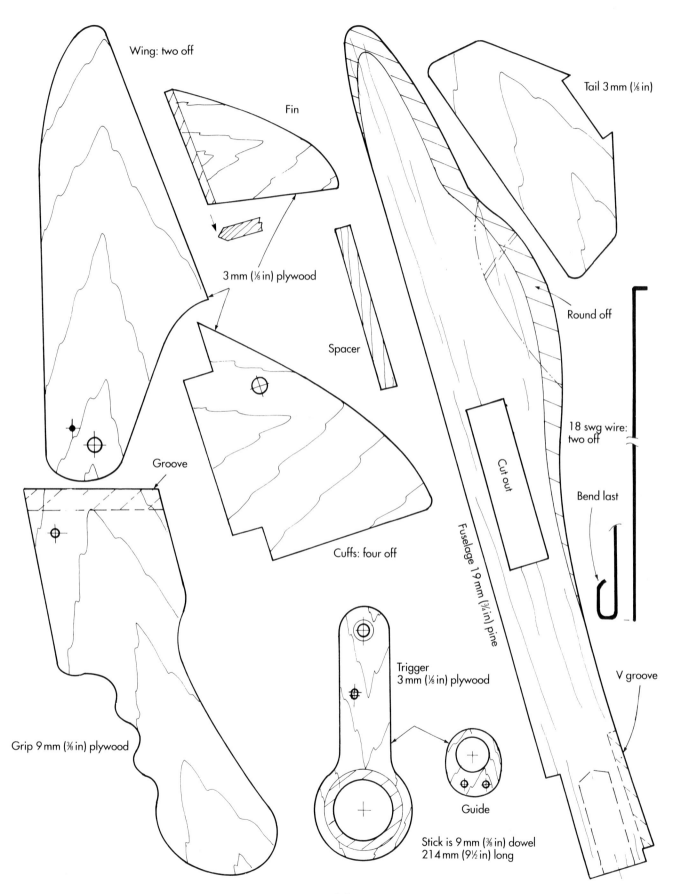

Wing: two off

Fin

3 mm (⅛ in) plywood

Spacer

Tail 3 mm (⅛ in)

Round off

18 swg wire: two off

Bend last

Groove

Cut out

Cuffs: four off

Fuselage 19 mm (¾ in) pine

V groove

Grip 9 mm (⅜ in) plywood

Trigger 3 mm (⅛ in) plywood

Guide

Stick is 9 mm (⅜ in) dowel 214 mm (9½ in) long

ORBITER

Here is a good opportunity for interactive play. The little plane or spacecraft can be made to circle a pylon by moving a lever from side to side. It does this by gravity, as the pivot of its supporting wire is tilted from the vertical. Once the craft has started to move round, the lever has to be leaned gently in the direction of the next part of the flight, so the owner can be in constant control. Faster and faster goes the craft until only a tiny amount of lever movement is needed to keep it going. This is an effective way of training the youngster's reactions.

Look at Fig. 1. With the craft on the left, the lever is moved to the right. This tilts the pivot of the wire, so that the path taken by the craft is a tilted circle. It swings to the low side, but gaining impetus, it passes the lowest point and starts to rise again. Now, when the lever is moved to the left, the axis is tilted the other way (as in Fig. 2), thus lifting the craft to a new, higher position. All is once again downhill until the craft passes the starting-point, when you cause it to continue the circle by moving the lever back again. You can stop the craft and make it go backwards by holding the lever in one position for longer.

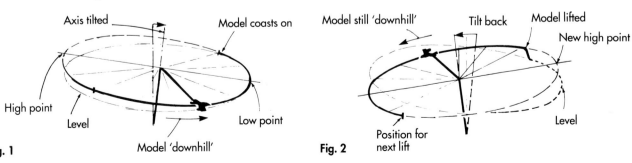

Fig. 1

Axis tilted

Model coasts on

High point

Level

Model 'downhill'

Low point

Fig. 2

Model still 'downhill'

Tilt back

Model lifted

New high point

Position for next lift

Level

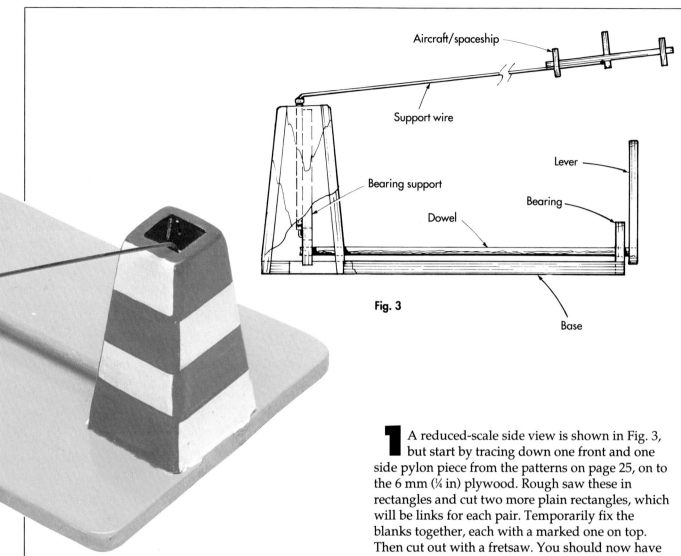

Aircraft/spaceship

Support wire

Bearing support

Lever

Bearing

Dowel

Fig. 3

Base

MATERIALS

3 mm (⅛ in) plywood:
   76 x 76 mm (3 x 3 in)
6 mm (¼ in) plywood:
   254 x 102 mm (10 x 4 in)
9 mm (⅜ in) plywood:
   203 x 153 mm (8 x 6 in)
6 mm (¼ in) dowel: 190 mm
   (7½ in)
1.5 mm (¹⁄₁₆ in) piano wire:
   381 mm (15 in)
Brass tube (or empty ball-pen
   ink tube): 64 mm (2½ in)
Carpet thread or flower wire
PVA glue
Fast epoxy glue
Paint

TOOLS

Hand saw
Fretsaw
Drill
Chisel
Snipe-nose pliers
Small file
Stanley knife
Paintbrushes
Rule
Pencil
Carbon paper

1 A reduced-scale side view is shown in Fig. 3, but start by tracing down one front and one side pylon piece from the patterns on page 25, on to the 6 mm (¼ in) plywood. Rough saw these in rectangles and cut two more plain rectangles, which will be links for each pair. Temporarily fix the blanks together, each with a marked one on top. Then cut out with a fretsaw. You should now have the makings of a square pylon. Take off any whiskers from the cut edges, and glue the sides between front and back panels. Use a scrap piece of square wood that will fit inside the top (narrow) end to hold it square, while you secure the joints with masking tape before the glue sets (Fig. 4).

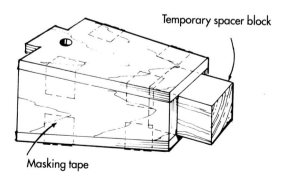

Temporary spacer block

Masking tape

Fig. 4

2 Bend the wire with pliers to form the support arm and pivot. Use the shape shown on the pattern page to check the end bends, but do not make the small bend at the bottom end yet. Cut a couple of thin slices from the tube to serve as spacing washers. You can do this with a Stanley knife, rolling the tube to and fro as in Fig. 5.

Slide the three pieces of tube on to the wire as per the pattern page and form the bottom bend. Check that the long tube spins freely between the spacers, then secure the spacers to the wire with fast epoxy.

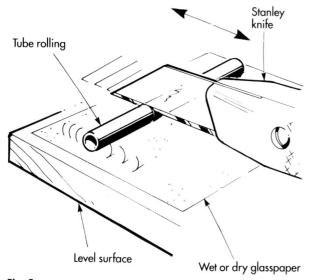

Fig. 5

3 While the epoxy sets, cut the bearing support, ready to mount the bearing tube. Then mark out from the pattern and cut the base panel. Remove the tape from the now dry pylon and shave the lugs of the pylon (Fig. 6), and the rebates in the base so that they match the angle of the pylon front and back (Fig. 7). This is shown in section in Fig. 8.

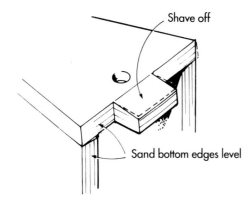

Fig. 6

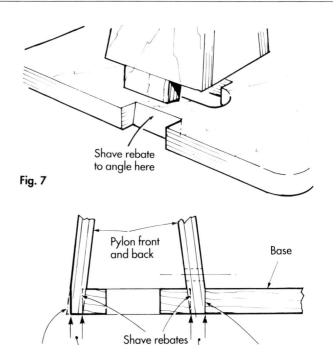

Fig. 7

Fig. 8

You can also make the lever and its support in 6 mm (¼ in) ply and glue the latter and the pylon into their rebates in the base.

4 The bearing should now be ready to fit (Fig. 9). Position it on the bearing support so that the bottom bend is over the clearance hole. Use carpet thread or flower wire to bind and sew the tube to the support, as shown in Fig. 10. Reinforce the joint with fast epoxy.

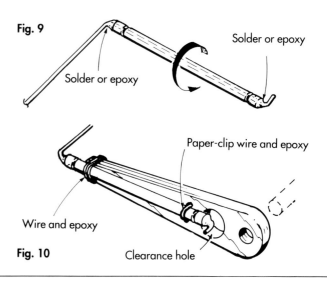

Fig. 9

Fig. 10

5 Mark out and cut all the parts for the spacecraft from 3 mm (⅛ in) plywood. Sand them, then glue them together as in Fig. 11. Epoxy the wire, as shown, under the wing.

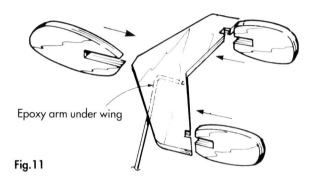

Epoxy arm under wing

Fig.11

6 Give the whole set of parts a final sanding and paint the model prior to the last part of the assembly.

7 Glue the lever on one end of the dowel shaft, and thread the latter through the lever support and the front of the pylon. Apply a little fast epoxy to the hole in the bottom of the bearing support, where the dowel is to go. Look underneath and insert the bearing assembly through the top of the pylon. Guide the dowel into the hole and hold the bearing vertical while twisting the level vertical too . . . That's it. The toy works best on a level surface.

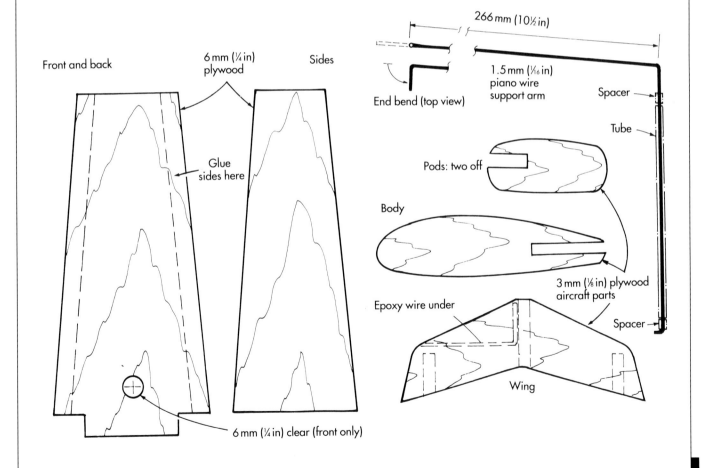

Front and back

6 mm (¼ in) plywood

Sides

Glue sides here

6 mm (¼ in) clear (front only)

266 mm (10½ in)

End bend (top view)

1.5 mm (¹⁄₁₆ in) piano wire support arm

Spacer

Tube

Pods: two off

Body

3 mm (⅛ in) plywood aircraft parts

Spacer

Epoxy wire under

Wing

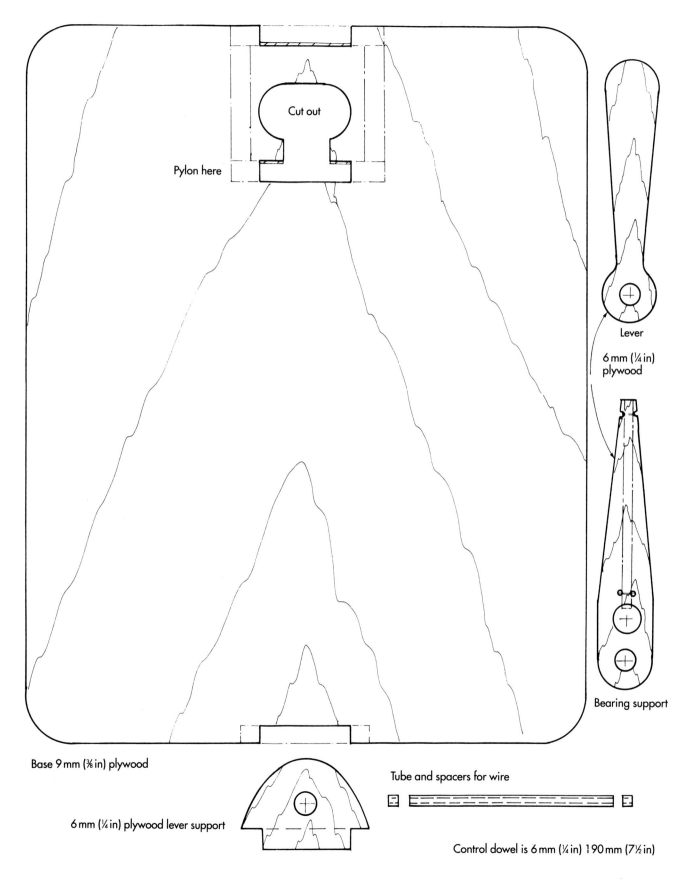

Cut out

Pylon here

Lever

6 mm (¼ in)
plywood

Bearing support

Base 9 mm (⅜ in) plywood

6 mm (¼ in) plywood lever support

Tube and spacers for wire

Control dowel is 6 mm (¼ in) 190 mm (7½ in)

Wheels with a jigsaw

Only the largest wheels can be made this way. Jigsaws intended for DIY jobs are not so suited for cutting tiny shapes from very small pieces of wood. True, they will do it if the wood is large and well clamped – then the saw can be moved without hitting any of the latter – so if you want to try, make the jig shown in Fig. 1. Use hard 6 mm (¼ in) or thicker plywood and put a fine tooth, narrow blade in the hand-held jigsaw. (It would be a different matter if you had an adaptor to enable the saw to be mounted in a proper saw table, blade upwards with a suitable guard, but I am dealing with the small, occasional use of the saw.)

How you secure the jig to the sole plate of the saw will depend on the make of tool, so those large screws and washers in Fig. 1 may be better replaced by countersunk bolts and nuts to clamp two metal plates (as shown in Fig. 2).

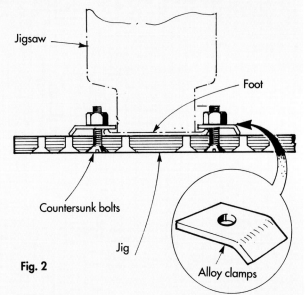

Fig. 2

Jigsaw

Foot

Countersunk bolts

Jig

Alloy clamps

Using the jig
Clamp the wood (as shown in Fig. 3) in a vice or the Workmate. The clamps must not protrude above the top surface of the wood, if the saw passes close to them. Set the notch in the jig at right angles to the blade, and the radius of the wheel from the side of the blade.

Start with the blade tangential to the wheel edge and advance the saw until the notch engages on a dowel pushed into the axle hole. At this point, the jig takes over. Allow it to turn the saw in a complete circle, as you follow by supporting the jigsaw against vibration.

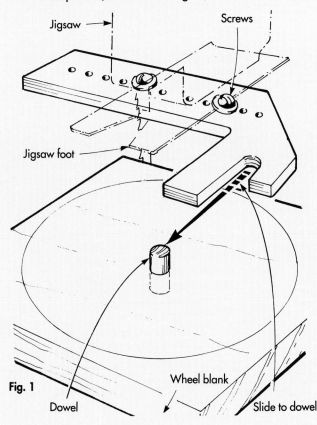

Fig. 1

Jigsaw

Screws

Jigsaw foot

Dowel

Wheel blank

Slide to dowel

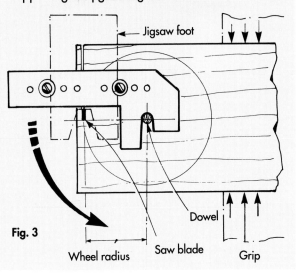

Fig. 3

Jigsaw foot

Dowel

Wheel radius

Saw blade

Grip

FLAPPING GOOSE

The push toy with flapping wings has always been a favourite. However, many examples use external wire links between the wings and screws or bolts in the outside of the wheels. This type may be quick to make, but eventually it is prone to failure due to the toy being banged against steps and kerbs, which knocks back the wire and bolt or whatever, preventing the wheels turning smoothly. The goose in this project has eccentrics on the inner face of the wheels, right against the body, where they are out of harm's way. Both eccentrics are in phase, so that the wires move in unison (see Fig. 1). The wings are hinged on a common wire support over the body. The wire springs taken from spring clothes-pegs are excellent for the job. They fit on to the wire and you bond them to the ply with epoxy glue.

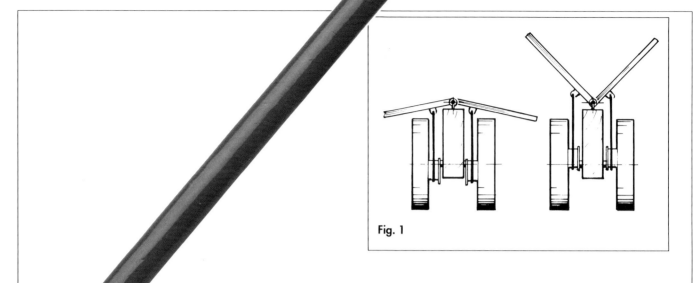

Fig. 1

MATERIALS

0.8 mm (1/32 in) plywood or
    Formica: 64 x 32 mm
    (2½ x 1¼ in)
3 mm (1/8 in) plywood:
    114 x 140 mm (4½ x 5½ in)
6 mm (¼ in) plywood:
    57 x 25 mm (2¼ x 1 in)
95 x 16 mm (3¾ x 5/8 in) pine:
    202 mm (8 in)
70 x 19 mm (2¾ x ¾ in) pine:
    254 mm (10 in)
6 mm (¼ in) dowel: 64 mm (2½ in)
12 mm (½ in) dowel: 355 mm
    (14 in)
1.5 mm (1/16 in) steel wire: 303 mm
    (12 in)
2 mm (3/32 in) steel wire: 127 mm
    (5 in)
Four springs from clothes-pegs
Two small staples
PVA glue
Fast epoxy glue
Body filler (optional)
Paint

TOOLS

Fretsaw (or
    coping-saw)
Drill
Hole saw
12 mm (½ in) flat
    bit
File
Hammer
Snipe-nose pliers
Glasspaper
Paintbrushes
Pencil
Carbon paper

The toy is shown in side view in Fig. 2. One wheel has been removed to show the eccentric on the axle and the link to the wings. Note the recess for the wings in the top of the body, and the clothes-peg springs, which do not provide spring action, but serve as hinges, by swivelling on the wire rod.

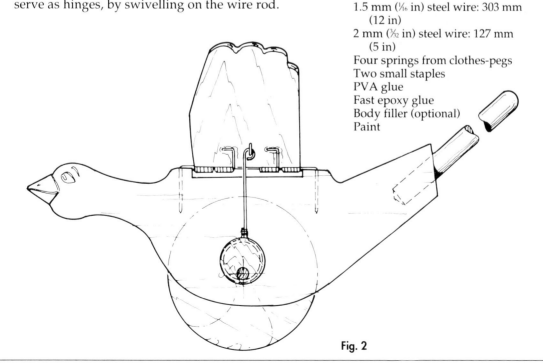

Fig. 2

1 Trace off the body shape from the template in page 32. Mark it on to the 19 mm (¾ in) pine. Drill the holes for the axle 6 mm (¼ in) clearance. Check the thicker wire size, and drill for a tight fit where shown. Do not push it in yet. With the body in a vice – to support it each side of the tail tip – drill with the flat bit to the depth shown dotted on the pattern. Go gently, as there is little wood to spare each side of the hole.

Make the handle, using the 12 mm (½ in) dowel. This will restore the strength; so glue it in at this stage, rather than later.

Round off the edges of the body and make the beak more (but bluntly) tapered in top view.

2 Mark the wing shape from the pattern on to 3 mm (⅛ in) plywood and fix a second rectangle of plywood below it. Use panel-pins to do this. Fret out the wings as one.

You will find that the peg springs will grip the ply. Slide them on to the inner end of each wing, so that one leg is above and one leg below. One wing should have the springs at the corners and the other has them spaced to fit between the others. See Fig. 3, where the wings are shown dotted. Slide the thick wire through all four spring coils and adjust the inner pair so that they touch the outer ones, yet allow the wings to move independently. Now fix them to the plywood with fast epoxy glue, but do not allow any glue to get on the coils of the springs. Just apply it to each L shape leg above and below, and allow it to harden.

3 Without disturbing the springs, withdraw the wire. Then, using either car body filler, or more epoxy glue plus fine sawdust, form a smooth patch at each wire and blend it into the wing surface (as in Fig. 4). The mixture must not go right over the coil.

Sand the wings; but before you set them aside for painting, bend one end of the wire at right angles (as the pattern), then thread it back through the spring coils. You will find that there is enough space to hold it with pliers at the other end, while you form the other bend. Temporarily push the wire into the body (as in Fig. 5) to test that the wings do not catch on the raised part of the body. The body has to prevent the wings sliding from end to end, so the springs or the plywood edges have to be just below the top. This means that you need to make small recesses, with a chisel or mouse-tail file, to house the wire.

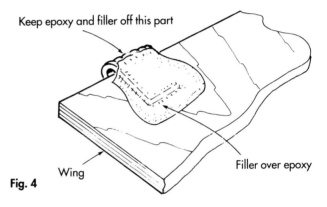

Keep epoxy and filler off this part

Wing

Filler over epoxy

Fig. 4

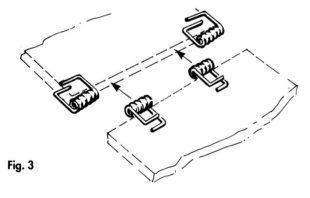

Fig. 3

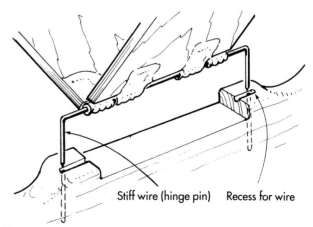

Stiff wire (hinge pin)   Recess for wire

Fig. 5

4 When you cut out the wheels with the fretsaw or coping-saw, it is best to drill the centre first; pop in a short crosshead screw, to just rest in the hole. Why? To hold the compass point, while you mark the outline of the rim. If you made the wheel first, then drilled it, the hole might be fractionally off-centre. This way, the hole controls the radius, whether you hold the wood by its centre on a screw, or saw it by eye to the line.

5 Fret out the pair of eccentrics, or use a hole saw. The latter will leave a hole in the centre. This does not matter. File or fret out a notch to allow the axle to lie flush with the edge, and glue it to the wheel. Make the thin ply retaining discs as a pair. If you substitute Formica, tape two pieces together on to a piece of thicker plywood, so that it does not chip as you saw it with a fine-tooth blade. Remember that the hole is set in from the edge, as the pattern shows. Never use a hole saw on small Formica or thin ply pieces: it may kick back. Do not glue these discs on yet.

6 Using the pattern as a guide, form an indentical pair of wire links. Bend the loop which goes around the eccentric, so that it slides smoothly but cannot slip off when the retaining discs are in position dry. Do not bind the loop ends yet, because it has to be opened a little to fit it later (see Fig. 6).

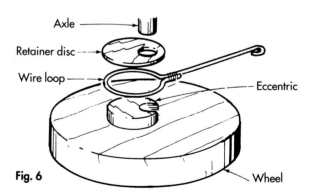

Fig. 6

7 Remove the wire. Glue the retaining discs on and glue the axle into one wheel/eccentric combination. Insert a small staple in each wing from below, as shown on the pattern. It will go right through, leaving enough loop to allow the link wire

small end to pass loosely. You can squeeze this to suit when you fit it later.

Using sharp pliers, end-cutters, or a file, trim the points off almost flush. Take the staple out, then glue it back in with fast epoxy (or cyano), as in Fig. 7. A smear of body filler will smooth the top of the wing here, if it looks untidy. Do not file the staple down completly flush. This may allow it to become loose with hard use.

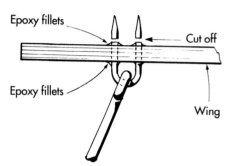

Fig. 7

8 Paint the whole toy in the part assemblies just described. When dry and hard, scrape away any paint from areas that have to be glued together. Free up the wing hinges and fix the wing wire in the body with fast epoxy. Slip each link over its eccentric and bind and epoxy the end, using the flower wire. Push the axle through the body and spin test for smoothness. Graphite pencil rubbed on makes a good lubricant. Put the other wheel, complete with eccentric and wire attached, on the free axle end and twist it so that both are up or down together (Fig. 1).

Lift each wing in turn and thread the link into the staple. You may have to tweak the small loops with the snipe-nose pliers to get them through and captive. All has to be free and rather loose; otherwise it may stick, until it is run-in.

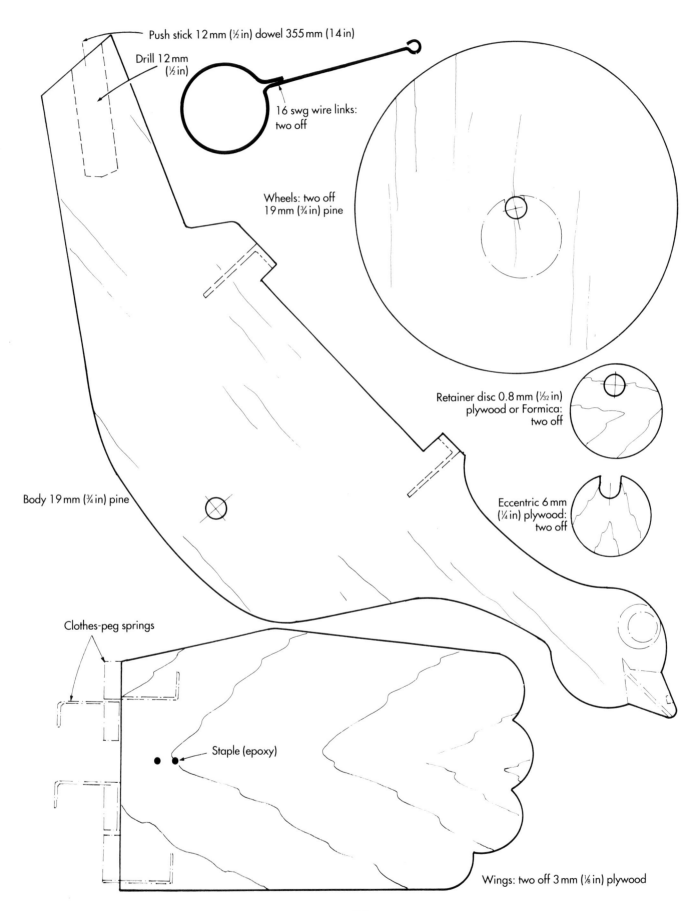

Push stick 12 mm (½ in) dowel 355 mm (14 in)

Drill 12 mm (½ in)

16 swg wire links: two off

Wheels: two off 19 mm (¾ in) pine

Retainer disc 0.8 mm (¹⁄₃₂ in) plywood or Formica: two off

Eccentric 6 mm (¼ in) plywood: two off

Body 19 mm (¾ in) pine

Clothes-peg springs

Staple (epoxy)

Wings: two off 3 mm (⅛ in) plywood

TIP

Wheels with a fretsaw

This involves marking out the wheels with a pencil compass. Suppose the wheel is large, and takes almost the full width of your wood. Find the centre and distance from the end by a pair of 45-degree lines from the end corners (as in Fig. 1). Smaller wheels can be staggered to save wood.

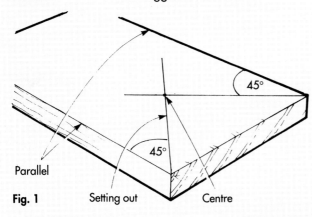

Parallel

Setting out

45°

45°

Centre

Fig. 1

Centre holes

It is quite possible to cut a nice round wheel, only to find that when you make the hole for the axle, it is not exactly in the centre. It is difficult to rectify this, other than re-cutting the edge and using it as a smaller wheel.

One solution is to make the hole first, then mark out the rim from this. However, the small compass point will float about in the axle hole, and even a small pilot hole leads to error. Fig. 2 shows that the axle hole drilled will take a cross-head screw that is a tight push fit. The centre of the cross holds the compass point.

Cutting jig

Recess a piece of thick plywood, so that a thin fretwork clamp will fit flush. Drill a series of pilot holes in the plywood and select one that brings the rim of the wheel close to an edge of the plywood. Use the cross-head screw to mount the workpiece to this, allowing it to rotate without wobbling. Slide the whole assembly about on the saw table to get the screw at right angles to the blade. Then tighten the clamp as you start (Fig. 4).

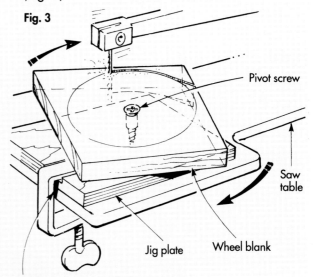

Fig. 3

Pivot screw

Saw table

Jig plate

Wheel blank

Fretwork clamp inset flush

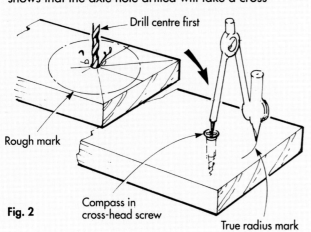

Drill centre first

Rough mark

Fig. 2

Compass in cross-head screw

True radius mark

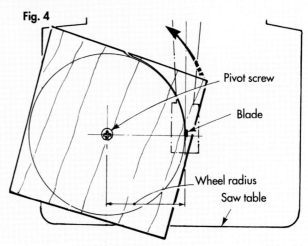

Fig. 4

Pivot screw

Blade

Wheel radius

Saw table

WALTZERS

This larger, pull-along toy is sure to make heads turn; in fact, both the dancers do rotate merrily as it is pushed or pulled. Their feet also jiggle as the toy bumps along. The drive is very simple (shown in Fig. 1). One of a pair of main wheels has a smaller drive wheel on its inner face. This turns a large horizontal disc which is attached to the dancers via a vertical dowel shaft. The legs hang loose on staples which are hidden inside the figures.

A pair of small bumper wheels are positioned fore and aft, so that most of the weight is available to help the main wheels to grip the ground. The section in Fig. 2 shows the general construction. It is not difficult to make, and you will enjoy finishing and painting the dancing couple.

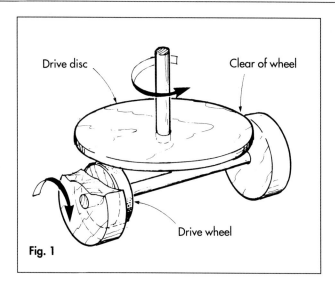

Fig. 1

Drive disc

Clear of wheel

Drive wheel

MATERIALS

6 mm (¼ in) plywood:
  355 x 125 mm (14 x 5 in)
9 mm (⅜ in) plywood:
  253 x 253 mm (10 x 10 in)
15 mm (⅝ in) pine: 127 x 64 mm
  (5 x 2½ in)*
19 mm (¾ in) pine: 127 x 102 mm
  (5 x 4 in)*
*large dimension grainwise
19 x 44 mm (¾ x 1¾ in) pine:
  419 mm (16½ in)
6 mm (¼ in) dowel: 457 mm
  (18 in)
12 mm (½ in) dowel: 76 mm (3 in)
One 51 x 6 mm (2 x ¼ in) rubber
  band
Eight small staples
Small screw eye
String
PVA glue
Fast epoxy glue
Paint

TOOLS

Tenon-saw
Fretsaw
Chisel
Drill
12 mm (½ in) flat
  bit
Hole saw
Rat-tail file
Hammer
Snipe-nose pliers
Sandpaper
Try-square
Rule
Pencil
Carbon paper
Paintbrushes

1 Study Fig. 2 and the cross-section in Fig. 3, which show the arrangement of the components. Then start with a spot of work on the 19 x 44 mm (¾ x 1¾ in) pine.

Saw it in the centre to make a pair of sides for the base. Check and mark the shapes of the cut-outs and rebates from the patterns on pages 38–40. Use the tenon-saw and chisel to form these features. Note that only one piece has a recess in the side for the drive wheel, but both have recesses to clear the drive disc in the top edges.

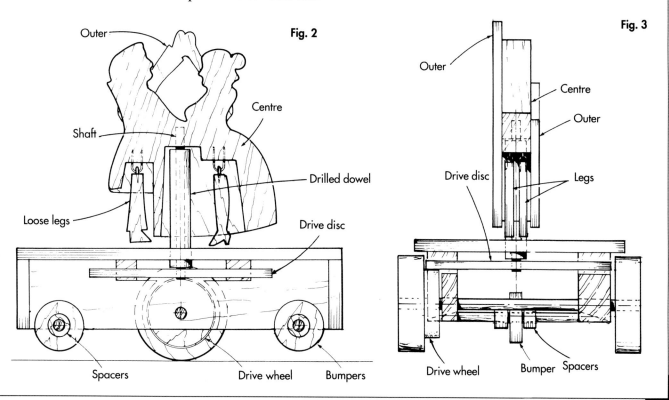

Fig. 2

Outer

Centre

Shaft

Drilled dowel

Loose legs

Drive disc

Spacers

Drive wheel

Bumpers

Fig. 3

Outer

Centre

Outer

Drive disc

Legs

Drive wheel

Bumper

Spacers

2 Next, mark out and cut the base top and ends (9 mm/⅜ in) plywood. Sand the top edges of the side pieces, and de-whisker all the edges of the top and ends. Check for fit, remembering that the sides of the top are intended to overhang the side pieces. Glue the ends into the rebates in the ends of the sides, but do not glue the top to any of the four pieces yet. Just rest it on dry to keep things level. Put a clamp each side to hold the sides to the ends, and put a weight on the top.

3 While the base is drying, tackle the dancers. Trace down on to the 19 mm (¾ in) pine the core shape of the figures. Mark the areas that you have to chamfer off, but do not carve yet. Also trace off the outer laminations of the figures (6 mm/¼ in) plywood. Note which way they go from Fig. 4, then glue one outer in place, matching the curves to the core. When dry, put in four small temporary staples upon which to hang the legs, then loosen them (it is easier at this stage).

Drill between the figures as shown on the template, to take a 6 mm (¼ in) dowel. Try not to let the hole break out at the top. Now glue on the other outer piece. When dry, carefully pare away the areas of chamfer with a chisel. There is no need to carve features: these figures are stylized, squared-off works of art!

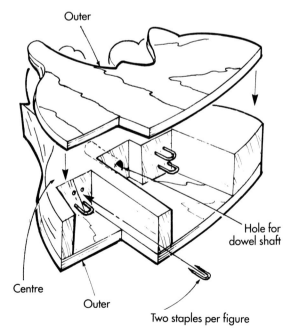

Outer

Hole for dowel shaft

Centre

Outer

Two staples per figure

Fig. 4

4 Measure from the pattern and mark out the drive disc on to 6 mm (¼ in) plywood. Cut this with the fretsaw and drill perfectly in the centre to take the 6 mm (¼ in) shaft dowel. Glue the shaft in, using a pair of 90-degree checking squares of card or a pair of small try-squares. As shown in Fig. 5, it is important that the disc spins without a wobble.

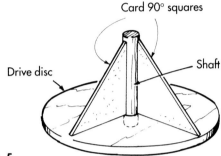

Card 90° squares

Drive disc

Shaft

Fig. 5

5 Drill the 12 mm (½ in) dowel right through its length to clear a 6 mm (¼ in) dowel. This is a slow and careful job. Keep checking that the drill is vertical while holding the dowel in a vice. Avoid pinching it too tightly, though, or the hole will not be round. You may be able to sense if the drill is getting ready to break out sideways. If so, turn the job over and go in from the other end. That hole has to be a free fit on the dowel you put in the disc, so it may need freeing up with a rat-tail file.

6 When you are quite satisfied that all is free and smooth, drill the 12 mm (½ in) hole in the centre of the base top with a flat bit, and glue in the dowel. Use the pair of card pieces as before to get

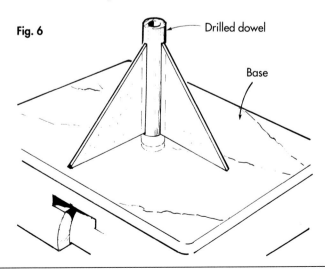

Fig. 6

Drilled dowel

Base

the thing really upright. Rest the top back on the base sides, still dry, while you do this (Fig. 6). You can also put the shaft and disc in the tubular dowel and with the base top on its sides, check that it does not catch on the recesses you cut earlier. If you get the all clear, glue the top on. This is the last chance you will get to adjust the disc or the top.

7 Mark out and cut the legs. You can do these in pairs to maintain accuracy. File small notches in the tops of each leg (as in Fig. 7) so that you can fix a staple in place with epoxy.

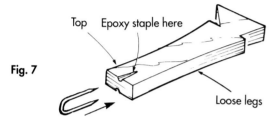

Top   Epoxy staple here

Fig. 7

Loose legs

8 Make all the wheels and the spacers for the fore and aft bumper types. A hole saw with various blades will help you to do the wheels speedily. Remember the tips on page 55. Check each for wobble-free fitting on their dowel axles. The spacers are best cut with a fretsaw, after drilling. Glue the drive wheel to one main wheel and add the rubber band for friction. Use epoxy to keep it in place, but keep the epoxy off the outside.

9 Painting is best done now, so prepare each part by fine sanding, filling and getting a good gloss finish. See the chapter on page 114, dealing with the painting stages which apply to all the projects. See Fig. 10 for suggestions on painting the faces.

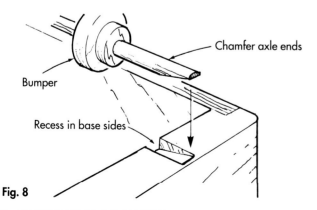

Chamfer axle ends

Bumper

Recess in base sides

Fig. 8

10 Thread the main axle through, and glue the wheels on. File notches in the sides, where shown, to take the bumper axles. Chamfer these and, after threading on and gluing a spacer each side of each bumper wheel, shave a chamfer on each end to help the axle to fit into the notches. Fig. 8 explains.

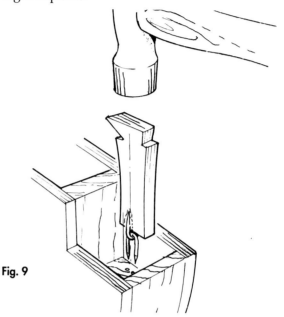

Fig. 9

11 Hold the figures, head downwards, in a vice with cloth padding to prevent damage to the paint. Reach inside with snipe-nose pliers and pull out the staples you put in earlier (this was to mark their position and to make sure they went back easily). Hook each staple through the one epoxied on the leg. Put a tiny spot of fast epoxy on each of its points. Dangle it down into the holes it left, and tap the foot of the leg with a small hammer (as in Fig. 9). This will hold each leg in position.

Fig. 10

12 Glue the figures on to the top of the pivot dowel, with the feet only just clear of the top surface of the base. Fit a screw hook and string to one end, and go waltzing.

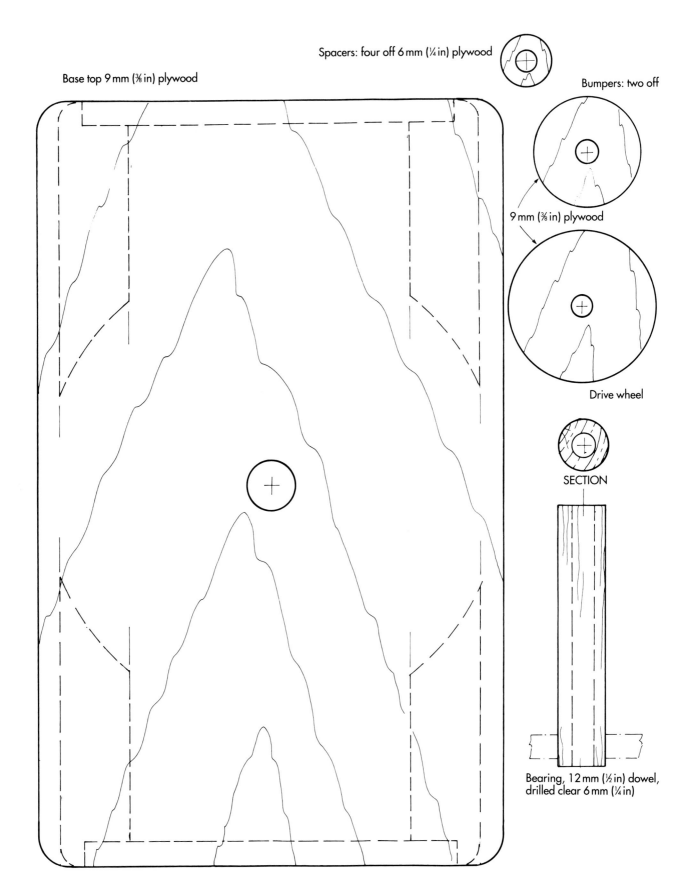

Spacers: four off 6 mm (¼ in) plywood

Base top 9 mm (⅜ in) plywood

Bumpers: two off

9 mm (⅜ in) plywood

Drive wheel

SECTION

Bearing, 12 mm (½ in) dowel,
drilled clear 6 mm (¼ in)

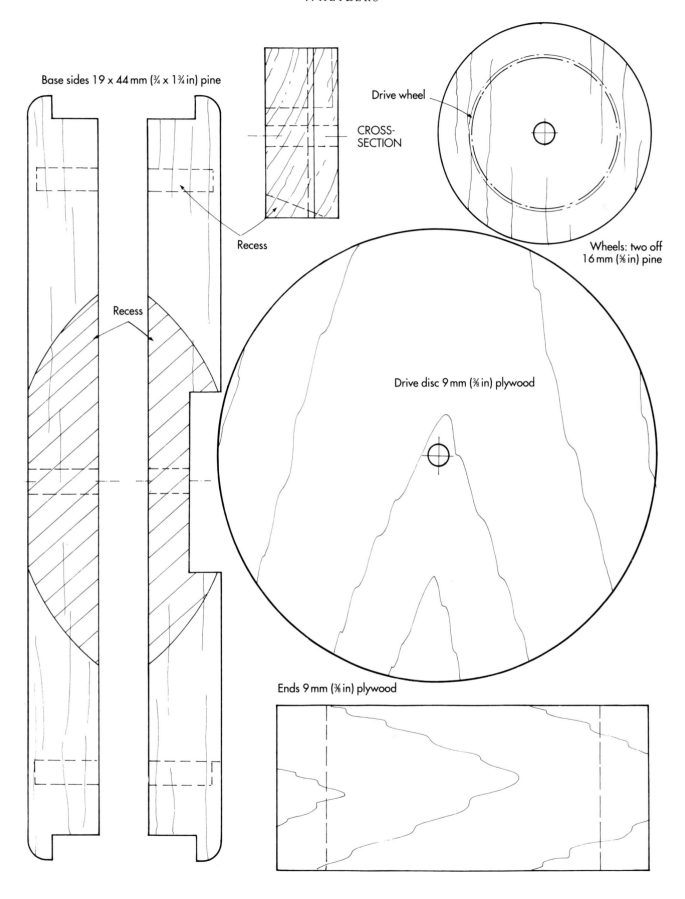

Base sides 19 x 44 mm (¾ x 1¾ in) pine

CROSS-SECTION

Recess

Recess

Drive wheel

Wheels: two off
16 mm (⅝ in) pine

Drive disc 9 mm (⅜ in) plywood

Ends 9 mm (⅜ in) plywood

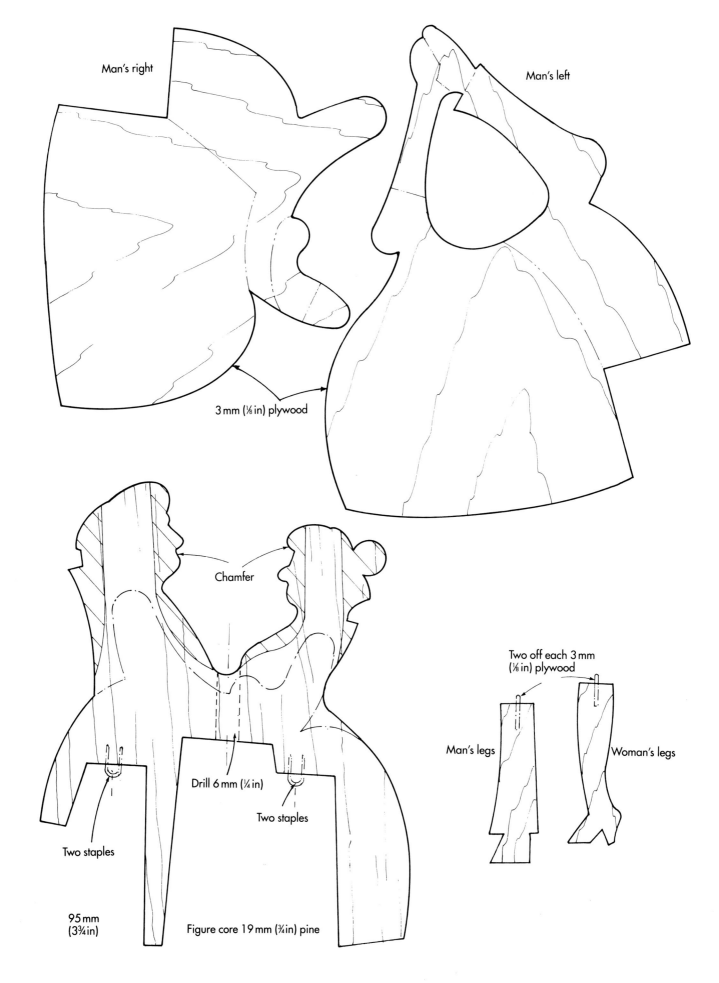

Man's right

Man's left

3 mm (⅛ in) plywood

Chamfer

Two off each 3 mm (⅛ in) plywood

Man's legs

Woman's legs

Drill 6 mm (¼ in)

Two staples

Two staples

95 mm (3¾ in)

Figure core 19 mm (¾ in) pine

TIP

Smooth bearings

Wood-on-wood, the traditional bearings for this type of toy, have to be really free if they are to turn and slide easily. Wood will shrink, or even warp under adverse conditions. Imagine a good-fitting dowel in a straight hole. Fine when first fitted, then the dowel warps, probably because of poor grain selection, or the wood through which the hole is drilled starts to cup or curl, due to natural shrinkage or one side being exposed to the heat of the sun while the other lies on wet grass. In either case, the toy will have to be taken apart and the hole or axle re-worked to accommodate the misalignment that has crept in. Now, a nicely finished wheel, on an axle that has to be replaced, is going to suffer. The axle has to be cut and drilled out – so that's a new paint job. It is no good having wheels press-fitted: the user will un-fit them. Some toys have wheels mounted on woodscrews, but these are also prone to come out dangerously, unless locked with epoxy, which may damage the wood when clouted hard, as might happen on a pull-along toy.

Drill the axle hole about 1 mm (³⁄₆₄ in) larger than the dowel size. This will allow for wood movement, yet not be so loose as to make the parts rattle unduly, or loose much drive effect when working something.

Never lubricate wood-to-wood bearings with oil: it swells the wood and collects dirt. On the other hand, graphite is excellent. Rub a pencil on a piece of glasspaper, and gather the dust on a pipe cleaner to insert into the hole if it is deep, or rub the pencil in the hole if it is shallow. Pencil on the dowels as well. This is a smooth-acting lubricant. See Fig. 3, which also shows talcum powder. This is loose, so it is easily tipped and blown into bearing holes and dusted on axles or shafts.

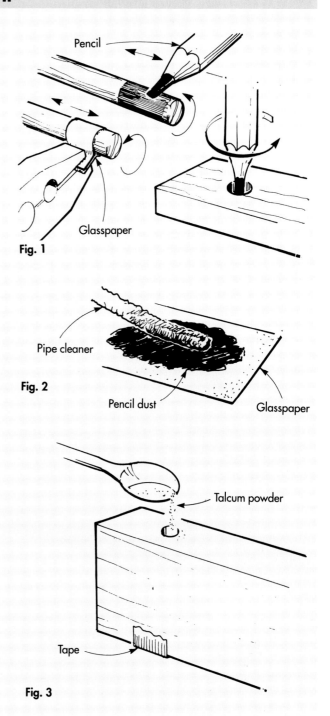

Fig. 1

Pencil

Glasspaper

Fig. 2

Pipe cleaner

Pencil dust

Glasspaper

Talcum powder

Tape

Fig. 3

THE SHIRT

Who will win: the goat or the farmer's wife? This parallelogram stick toy is at a large scale, for added impact. It is also less difficult to make than small items. Fig. 1 shows the method of operation. At first sight, it might be thought to be a standard two-figure toy, but the shirt connects them. So, in order to avoid a clash of movement, the goat drives the farmer's wife via the shirt. She is simply pivoted by her feet, with no direct linkage below, other than a coupling between the two sticks themselves, to maintain the parallelogram.
The whole toy is very simple to make.

MATERIALS

6 mm (¼ in) plywood:
    177 x 127 mm (7 x 5 in)
9 mm (⅜ in) plywood:
    165 x 140 mm (6½ x 5½ in)
19 x 6 mm (¾ x ¼ in) pine:
    610 mm (24 in)
Small scrap of 12 mm (½ in)
    dowel
Eight No. 6 countersunk 12 mm
    (½ in) woodscrews
Fast epoxy glue
Paint

TOOLS

Fretsaw
Drill
Screwdriver
Sandpaper
Paintbrushes
Pencil
Carbon paper

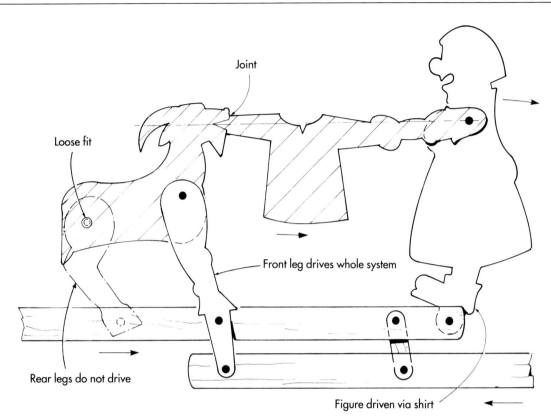

Joint

Loose fit

Front leg drives whole system

Rear legs do not drive

Figure driven via shirt

Fig. 1

1 Copy the shapes from the patterns on page 45 on to the plywood. Use carbon paper and a hard pencil. Keep the outlines close to the edge of the wood to avoid overlap of the shapes. Also mark the positions of any holes. But there is no need, at this stage, to copy the decoration. Be sure, however, to hold the paper to the wood with masking tape in a couple of places, so that it does not skid and change the shape in the process. Grease-proof paper is cheap and adequate for tracing from the page before taking it to the wood.

2 Cut the shapes out with a fretsaw. Note that there are pairs of goat legs. You can cut a separate rectangle for each and tack it with two panel-pins, each below the piece with the carbon outline on. Cut them two at a time with the fretsaw. If you are using a hand-frame tool, rather than a power fretsaw or scroll-saw, be careful to hold it with the blade really upright, otherwise the legs will be different sizes. Drill any holes in these double cutting pairs before you saw. This will ensure that they pivot in the right place. You will notice that one front leg does not need the extra link length. You can make one piece of plywood shorter, so that the

unwanted part is missed, or you can cut off the unwanted area afterwards.

The shirt is thinner than the goat's mouth, so it has to be glued in. Make sure that the angles match when you cut the mouth and the end of the shirt.

3 Sand the components to remove rough or hairy edges, and fix the shirt into the goat's mouth with fast epoxy. Lay the parts on a flat surface with a piece of polythene under the joint to prevent it sticking to the surface itself. It should be flush at the rear surface (Fig. 2).

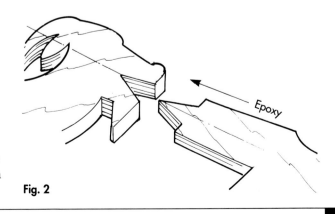

Epoxy

Fig. 2

4 The shirt already has the left arm incorporated. Now the right arm has to be joined to it via a spacing 'hand', otherwise the farmer's wife will look more unbalanced than she is already. This is where the scrap of 12 mm (½ in) dowel comes in. Cut it to length so that it fits between both hands and keeps the arms clear of the body . . . in other words more than 9 mm (⅜ in) long.

Drill the hole in the body to clear the woodscrew easily, which will go right through and bite into the right arm (see Fig. 3). Do not screw it together yet, because the sticks have to be made and connected.

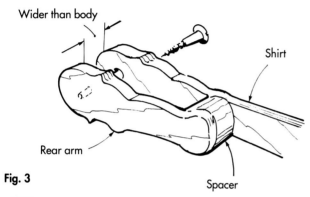

Fig. 3

5 Make the hole in the goat for its rear leg screw, really free – 5 mm (³⁄₁₆ in) will do. This is to prevent the geometry becoming restrictive. Temporarily screw the legs on with the screws free in the body, but firm into the *goat's* left legs (see the top view in Fig. 4).

6 Cut the pine strip into two equal lengths and measure the positions of holes from the templates page. Drill these clear for the goat's hooves, and the rest as pilot holes for the other screws. Mark them top and bottom and on the rear faces, according to the patterns. Consult Fig. 5 to check. Now, round off the ends with the fretsaw and sandpaper.

7 Take out the screws, and paint the components separately. If you try to paint parts that are meant to swivel, while they are screwed together, they will become stuck together; besides, they are more difficult to paint properly in that state.

8 When you have achieved a pleasing paint finish, clear the holes which have become clogged, and re-assemble; this time with the link and both sticks. Do not tighten the screws so much that the movement is stiff. If you find that any screw is in danger of loosening itself, take it out and put a tiny spot of fast epoxy on the extreme tip. This will bond it to the part where it has to bite, but not the free swivelling part. In addition, if the recipient is mechanically minded and curious, with a secret screwdriver to hand, foil those little tricks: fill the screw slots with epoxy and paint over them!

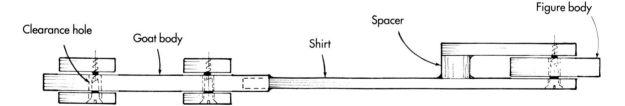

Fig. 4

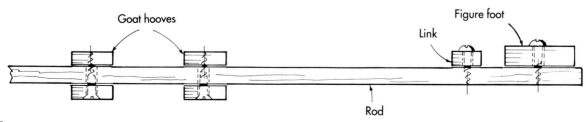

Fig. 5

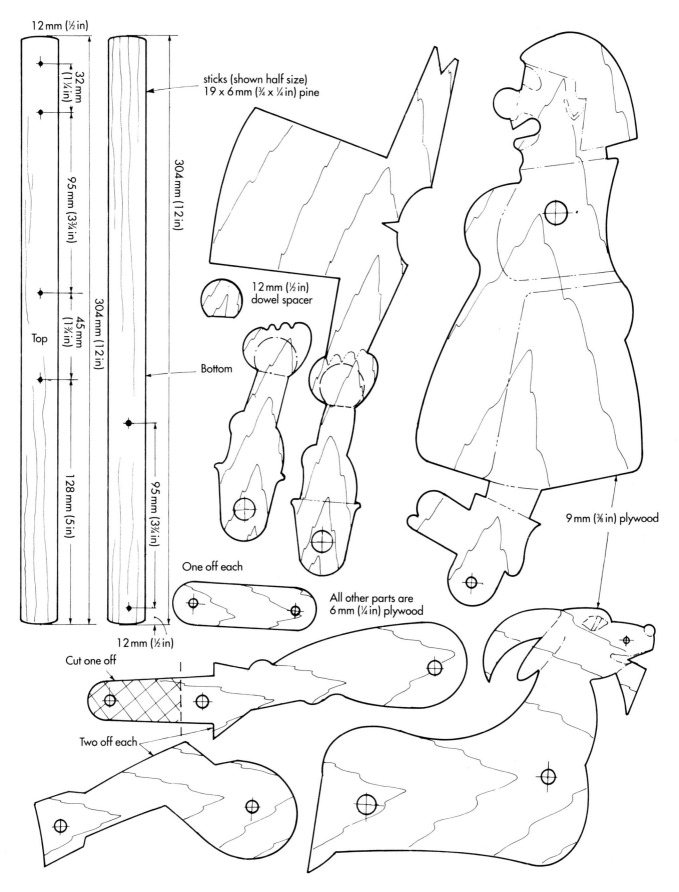

12 mm (½ in)

32 mm
(1¼ in)

95 mm (3¾ in)

304 mm (12 in)

Top

304 mm (12 in)

45 mm
(1¾ in)

128 mm (5 in)

sticks (shown half size)
19 x 6 mm (¾ x ¼ in) pine

12 mm (½ in)
dowel spacer

Bottom

95 mm (3¾ in)

One off each

12 mm (½ in)

All other parts are
6 mm (¼ in) plywood

9 mm (⅜ in) plywood

Cut one off

Two off each

45

TUG OF WAR

This, even larger, stick toy is rather like a production line, in that you make six bodies and twelve arms. The rest is even more simple than the Shirt. A push results in a win by the blue team and a pull gives their opponents the prize. Only the end-member of each team is connected to the lower stick. All the other figures are moved by the rope, which is in tension. Fig. 1 shows the side view when the sticks are pulled. Each team is inclined back slightly when at rest, so that the winners lean right back in the appropriate manner.

MATERIALS

5 mm (³⁄₁₆ in) plywood:
    178 x 102 mm (7 x 4 in)
9 mm (⅜ in) plywood:
    303 x 152 mm (12 x 6 in)
19 x 6 mm (¾ x ¼ in) pine:
    965 mm (38 in)
6 mm (¼ in) dowel: 127 mm (5 in)
12 mm (½ in) dowel: 64 mm
    (2½ in)
Eight 19 mm (¾ in) round-head
    woodscrews
White string
PVA glue
Fast epoxy glue
Paint

TOOLS

Fretsaw
Tenon-saw
Drill
Screwdriver
Sandpaper
Paintbrushes
Pencil
Carbon paper
Rule

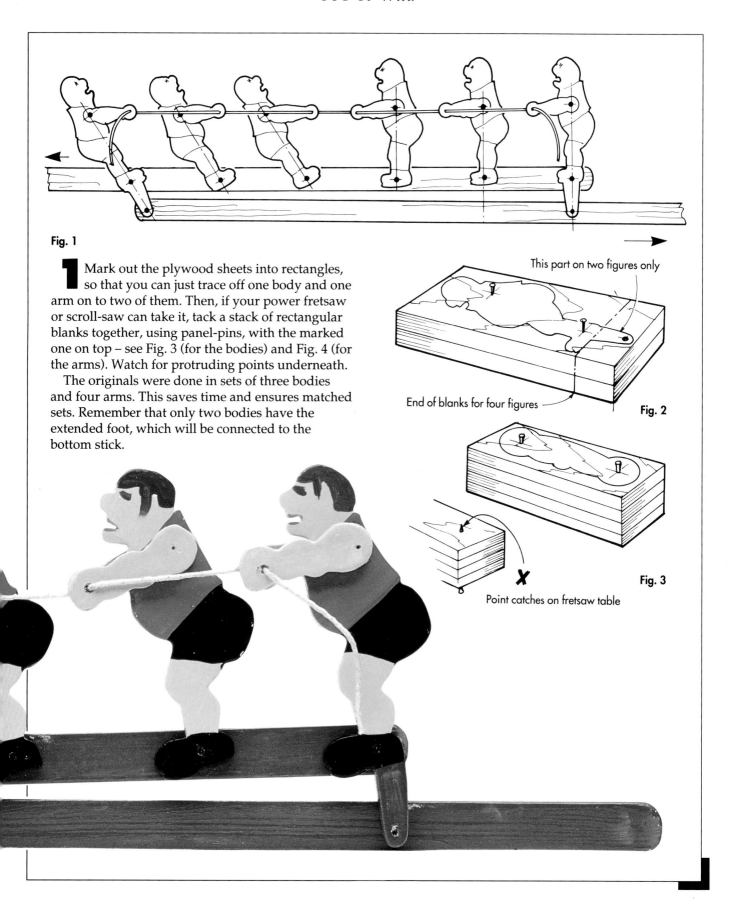

Fig. 1

1 Mark out the plywood sheets into rectangles, so that you can just trace off one body and one arm on to two of them. Then, if your power fretsaw or scroll-saw can take it, tack a stack of rectangular blanks together, using panel-pins, with the marked one on top – see Fig. 3 (for the bodies) and Fig. 4 (for the arms). Watch for protruding points underneath.

The originals were done in sets of three bodies and four arms. This saves time and ensures matched sets. Remember that only two bodies have the extended foot, which will be connected to the bottom stick.

This part on two figures only

End of blanks for four figures

Fig. 2

Point catches on fretsaw table

Fig. 3

Drill before cutting is the rule. The arm holes in the body have to clear easily the 6 mm (¼ in) dowel, which will join each left arm to its right. Those holes in the arms are, therefore, just 6 mm (¼ in) to grip the dowel for gluing.

2 Make a lengthwise saw cut with a tenon-saw on the 12 mm (½ in) dowel, then part it into slices just thicker than the 9 mm (⅜ in) body (as in Fig. 5). These are the hand spacers, and the saw cut is to allow the string to be threaded through. Glue one to each rear arm; that is to say, the arms that will be on the opposite side to the string – the left team's left and the right team's right arms. Also glue a slice of 6 mm (¼ in) dowel into the opposite arm (see Fig. 6). Do not glue the arms together yet.

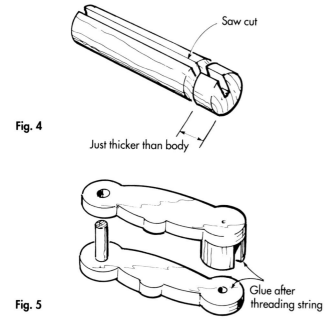

Fig. 4

Saw cut

Just thicker than body

Fig. 5

Glue after threading string

3 Cut the pine strip into equal lengths for the sticks. Drill to clear the screws, and shape the ends. Temporarily screw on the two-end figures and test to check that the parallelogram action works. Take it apart and prepare for painting.

4 When painting the arms, keep the area clear where the dowel spacers have to meet the front arms, or at least be prepared to scrape it clear as you go. The glue does not bond well to paint and much clogging here will also prevent the string being threaded easily later.

5 Pivot all the figures to the sticks loosely with the screws. Insert all the front arms, by passing the dowels through the bodies. Then attach a piece of string to the left end-figure's hand, by passing it through the hole and pulling back a length to trail at his feet. Take the long end and thread it in turn from behind each hand and through from the front of the next, until you get to the centre pair. Connect inside to inside and continue on to the figure at the opposite end. The top view of the threading is shown in Fig. 7; also shown is the component parts of the arms and spacers for earlier reference.

Slide each figure along the string, and tighten the latter until all figures are evenly spaced and there is no appreciable slack in it. Now, with a spot of PVA glue on a matchstick, glue the string to the hole in each front hand. Then glue on the rear arms at the dowels, and the spacers at both ends. The slots in the spacers should straddle the string, as it goes from hand to hand.

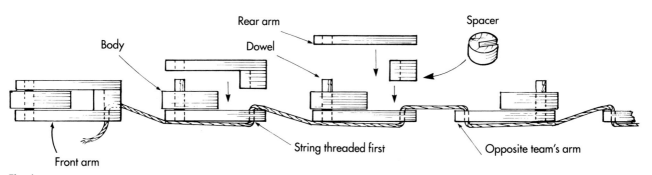

Body

Rear arm

Dowel

Spacer

Front arm

String threaded first

Opposite team's arm

Fig. 6

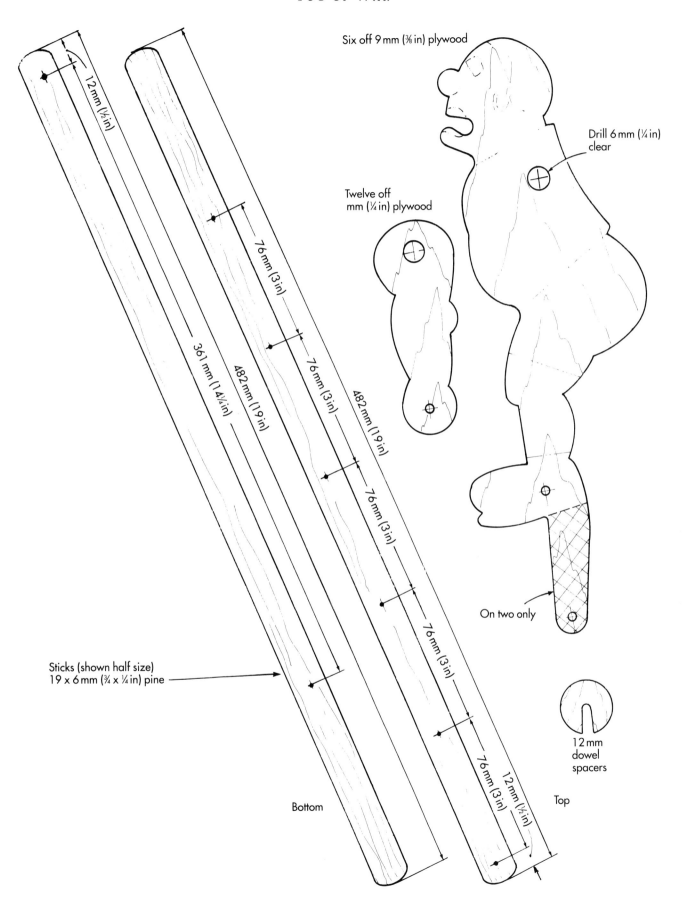

Six off 9 mm (⅜ in) plywood

Drill 6 mm (¼ in) clear

Twelve off mm (¼ in) plywood

On two only

12 mm (½ in)

76 mm (3 in)

76 mm (3 in)

482 mm (19 in)

482 mm (19 in)

361 mm (14¼ in)

76 mm (3 in)

76 mm (3 in)

76 mm (3 in)

12 mm (½ in)

12 mm dowel spacers

Sticks (shown half size)
19 x 6 mm (¾ x ¼ in) pine

Bottom

Top

TROUSERS DOWN!

This simple, plywood standing puppet is a silhouette figure plugged into a supporting block of wood. Pull a thin string and he lifts his arms, as if to fly, but whoops! his smart check trousers do a crash landing about his ankles, showing off traditional polka-dot underwear (below, right). Release the string and his arms drop as if to grab his trousers, but they are too quick for him and rise gracefully to their original position (as in Fig. 1). Move his arms alternately by taking him by the hand and those elusive trousers do a rumba. The action depends on the arms being heavier than the trousers, so you make these from thick plywood, and chose a thin, light type for the trousers.

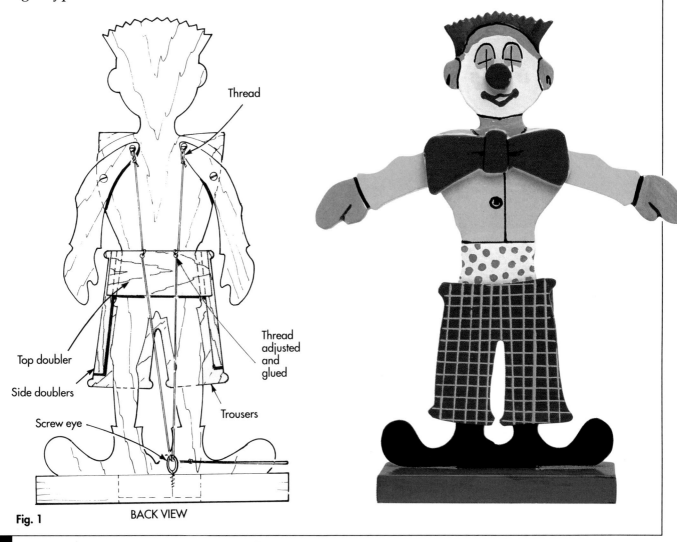

Thread

Top doubler

Side doublers

Screw eye

Thread adjusted and glued

Trousers

Fig. 1

BACK VIEW

MATERIALS

1.5 mm (¹⁄₁₆ in) plywood: 101 x 101 mm
    (4 x 4 in)
3 mm (⅛ in) plywood: 270 x 140 mm
    (10⅝ x 5½ in)
9 mm (⅜ in) plywood: 101 x 76 mm
    (4 x 2¾ in)
12 x 51 mm (½ x 2 in) pine: 133 mm
    (5¼ in) long
Two countersunk No. 4 15 mm
    (⅝ in) woodscrews
Two No. 2 10 mm (⅜ in) round-
    head woodscrews
One small screw eye
Strong carpet thread
PVA glue
Paint

TOOLS

Fretsaw, hand or
    machine
Tenon-saw
Chisel
Hand or electric
    drill
Countersink
Mouse-tail file
Small screwdriver
Medium and fine
    glasspaper
Paintbrushes
Pencil
Carbon paper
Rule
Scissors

1 Cut the small piece of thickest plywood lengthwise to make a pair of rectangular blanks for the arms. Tape them together to form a double thickness. Copy the arm outline from the patterns on page 54, as shown in Fig. 2. It does not matter if the tape gets in the way, draw over it; but remember to mark the hole positions and drill them before doing any cutting. The smallest hole is less than 1.5 mm (1/16 in), so take care. Both holes have to be vertical, so that they match both arms. Clean up any rough edges underneath, or they will snag on the table and cause the blade to jerk.

Fig. 2

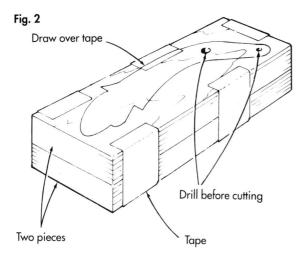

Draw over tape

Drill before cutting

Two pieces

Tape

2 Now cut out the outline to produce an exact pair of arms. The power fretsaw will do the job vertically, but it is up to you with a hand frame! You will find that the arms stay together as the outline is nearly finished, because the wood around it can be gripped. See Fig. 3.

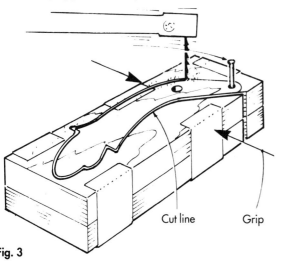

Cut line

Grip

Fig. 3

3 Having freed the arms, turn one over so that you have a left and right pair. Countersink the large hole in each, as in Fig. 4. You can use a hand or drill bit type of countersink.

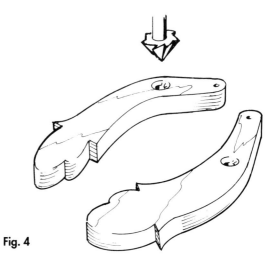

Fig. 4

4 Trace down the body, nose and tie outlines on to the 3 mm (1/8 in) plywood and fret them out. Glue the nose and tie in place where shown, but make sure that the edges are smooth first. You will find that the spiky hair can be cleaned up with a chisel. Drill 1.5 mm (1/16 in) pilot holes from the back of the body for the arm screws, but do not go right through.

5 Copy the trousers from the patterns on to the 1.5 mm (1/16 in) plywood, leaving lots of space

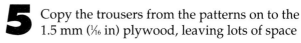

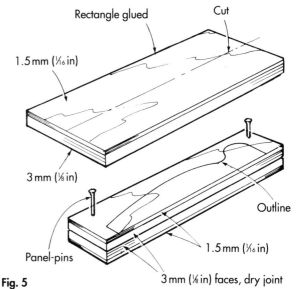

Rectangle glued

Cut

1.5 mm (1/16 in)

3 mm (1/8 in)

Panel-pins

Outline

1.5 mm (1/16 in)

3 mm (1/8 in) faces, dry joint

Fig. 5

to one side. Cut out the trousers and top doubler piece. You will be left with two spare pieces of plywood, one thin and one 3 mm (⅛ in). Cut each into a rectangle; then glue them together to form a thicker piece, as shown in Fig. 5. When set, saw it down the centre, trace the doubler outline on one, place it on top of the other, hold them together dry, with panel-pins as shown, and fret them out as a pair.

6 Glue one of these doublers to each edge of the trousers to act as spacers. When set, lay the body face down on the trousers (as in Fig. 6) and tape the top doubler across to retain it, while you check that the trousers slide up and down. Do not glue it on yet, because it will be difficult to paint the body with the trousers in place.

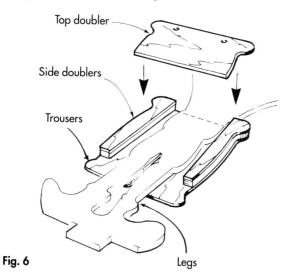

Top doubler

Side doublers

Trousers

Legs

Fig. 6

7 Trim the pine strip to size and form a recess for the body by drilling, and clean up with a chisel, as shown in Fig. 7. Sand all smooth prime, paint and enamel all the parts on their exposed faces.

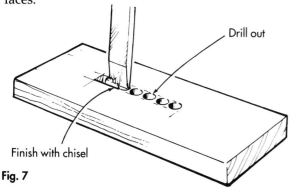

Drill out

Finish with chisel

Fig. 7

8 Following Fig. 8, and working from the back, screw the arms in place to pivot loosely. Glue the body into the base, and fit the trouser top doubler to hold the latter in place. Then, with the small remaining screws in the arms, rig the thread through the holes in the doubler as shown. Adjust until the trousers are up when the arms are down. Add the screw eye and pass the ends of the thread through it. A small bead on the end finishes it off.

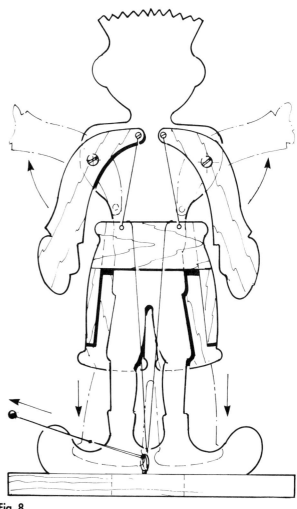

Fig. 8

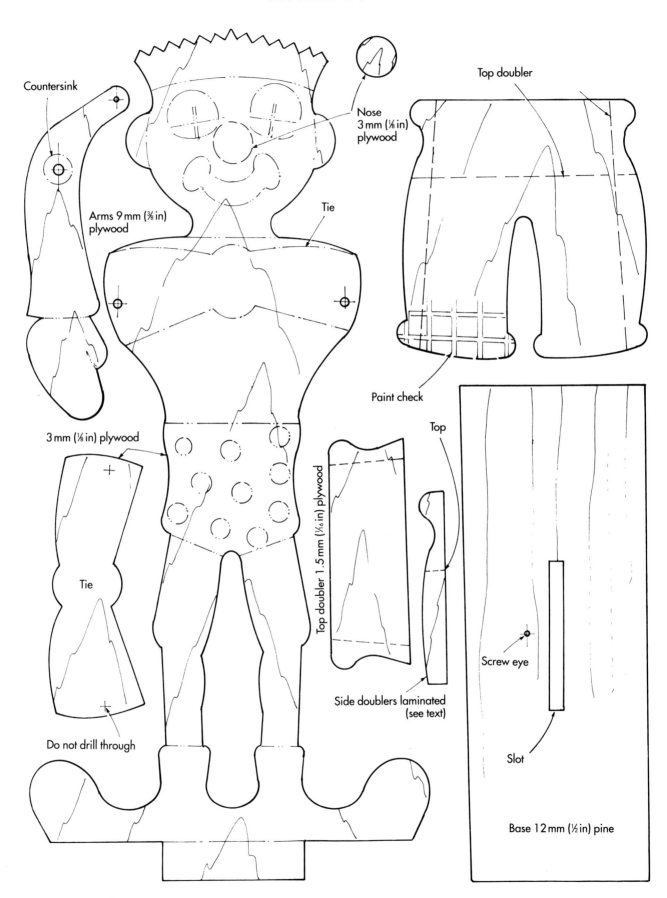

Countersink

Nose
3 mm (⅛ in)
plywood

Top doubler

Arms 9 mm (⅜ in)
plywood

Tie

Paint check

3 mm (⅛ in) plywood

Top doubler 1.5 mm (¹⁄₁₆ in) plywood

Top

Tie

Screw eye

Do not drill through

Side doublers laminated
(see text)

Slot

Base 12 mm (½ in) pine

TIP

Wheels with a hole saw

One of the quickest methods of making small wheels is to use a hole saw on your electric drill. Described among the tools, it will make large holes. But what about the middle of the hole? That is the wheel, already drilled to fit the axle. The hole saw comes with a selection of hacksaw-like cutter blades. Select the one that is nearest to the size of wheel that you need, by measuring the inner edge of the blade when it is in place.

In a stand

The drill is best mounted in a drill stand, so that it is firmly held in a vertical position. The lever which feeds the drill down gives you smooth control. This is important, because if the saw breaks through the other side suddenly, the wood may have splinters.

Fig. 1 shows how to set up the drill. The wood from which you will cut the wheels is centred on the stand. Set the depth limit on the stand so that the saw stops at half the thickness of the wood.

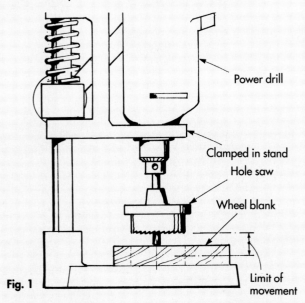

Power drill

Clamped in stand

Hole saw

Wheel blank

Fig. 1

Limit of movement

If you make a small pilot hole right through the intended centre of the wheel, you can turn the wood over and cut the other half, to meet the first perfectly. The edge will be true and the hole for the axle straight.

Freehand

Suppose you do not have a drill stand? The important hint is to hold the drill as vertical as possible and have the wood clamped firmly. The larger the wood the easier this is, because you now need some scraps of thinner wood to stop the saw from breaking right through.

Fig. 2 shows how to fix them so that the body of the saw comes to rest on all three of them when you drill vertically. Turn the wood over after removing those spacer pieces, and enter from the other side until the saw cuts meet.

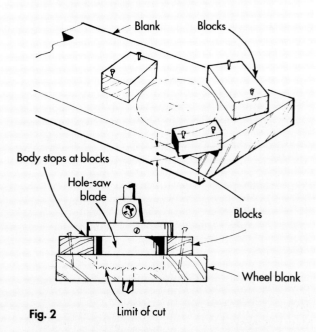

Blank

Blocks

Body stops at blocks

Hole-saw blade

Blocks

Wheel blank

Fig. 2

Limit of cut

The blocks will not correct a hole that starts really crooked, but you will see how the saw blade rests on the wood just before you ease it up a fraction to start the drill.

Fig. 3 shows what a mess you get if you try to straighten things out as you go.

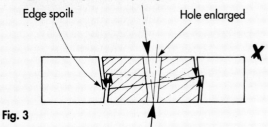

Edge spoilt

Hole enlarged

Fig. 3

Pogos

Pull this toy along, and two skinny figures bounce up and down, spinning round alternately. It is intended for the not-so-tiny tots, because it may not survive being thrown from a great height or mangled under a trundle toy. Were it more chunky, though, the mechanism would produce a less than sprightly effect. It is, however, a most interesting piece of friction and cam work which, although simple, gives two different actions. Ordinary cams (seen in Fig. 1) give a straight rise and fall, and it is usual to have the pushrod (which goes up and down) directly over the cam itself.

Now look at Fig. 2. The pushrod has a disc on the end, rather like that in Fig. 1, but the cam is offset to one side, so that it forms a friction drive. Now, as the cam rotates, it causes the pushrod to rotate as it rises and falls. This spins the figure. At the bottom, the cam clears the disc on the pushrod, so the figure takes a rest while his opposite number performs. The sectional view in Fig. 3 shows how the toy is assembled. A cross-section in Fig. 4 shows how the pushrod discs meet the cams.

In order to keep friction low, the figures are mounted through a thin plywood box. This minimizes the contact area on their pushrods. Both axles are held in grooved strips of wood under the base. These are called 'axle bars'.

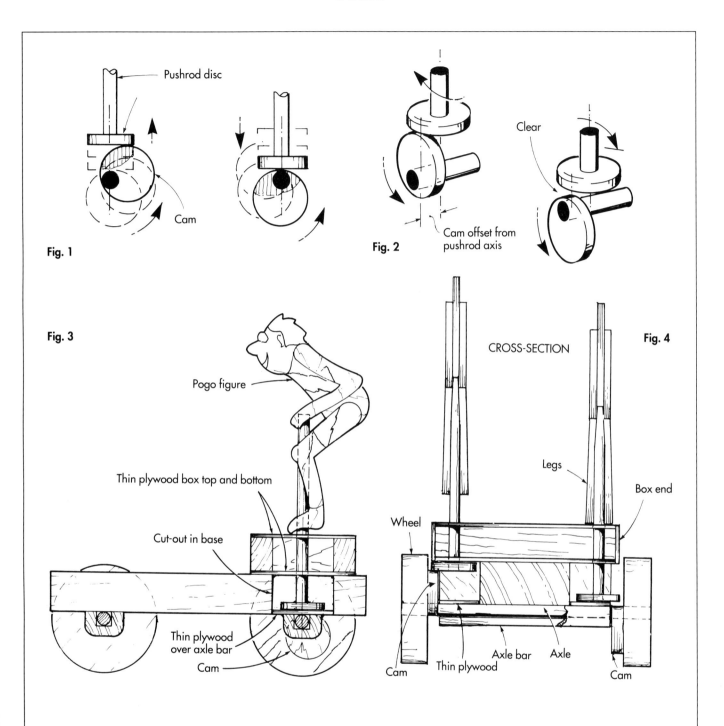

Fig. 1

Pushrod disc

Cam

Fig. 2

Clear

Cam offset from pushrod axis

Fig. 3

Pogo figure

Thin plywood box top and bottom

Cut-out in base

Thin plywood over axle bar

Cam

Fig. 4

CROSS-SECTION

Legs

Box end

Wheel

Cam

Thin plywood

Axle bar

Axle

Cam

MATERIALS

1.5 mm (1/16 in) plywood:
    165 x 101 mm (6½ x 4 in)
3 mm (⅛ in) plywood:
    202 x 152 mm (8 x 6 in)
6 mm (¼ in) plywood:
    51 x 25 mm (2 x 1 in)
19 x 12 mm (¾ x ½ in) pine:
    202 mm (8 in)

16 x 6 mm (⅝ x ¼ in) pine: 202 mm (8 in)
16 mm (⅝ in) pine: 254 x 64 mm
    (10 x 2½ in)
95 x 19 mm (3¾ x ¾ in) pine:
    171 mm (6¾ in)
6 mm (¼ in) dowel: 470 mm (18½ in)
PVA glue
Paint

TOOLS

Tenon-saw   Pencil
Fretsaw   Carbon paper
Chisel
Drill
Hole saw
Sandpaper
Paintbrushes
Try-square

1 Mark out the base and axle bars from the patterns on page 60. Using the tenon-saw and chisel, form the cut-outs in the base that are to house the pushrod discs.

Make lengthwise saw cuts in the pine strip that is to become the axle bars. Clean up the slots so formed to fit loosely on the 6 mm (¼ in) dowel that is to be used for the axles. Rest the bars against the base to see if the grooves are deep enough. Fig. 5 shows the detail at the rear end. There is a 1.5 mm (¹⁄₁₆ in) plywood rectangle to be cut to fit in the base cut-out. This is to support the rear axle at this point. Glue it to the axle bar and glue the latter to the base. Measure the position from the pattern.

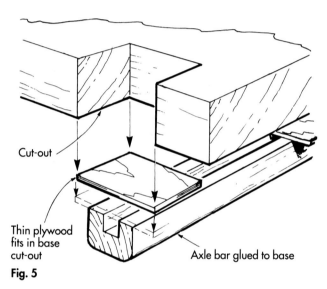

Cut-out

Thin plywood fits in base cut-out

Axle bar glued to base

Fig. 5

2 Cut the box top, bottom and ends from the rest of the 1.5 mm (¹⁄₁₆ in) plywood. You can measure the rectangles from the pattern page, and draw them on the plywood with a try-square and

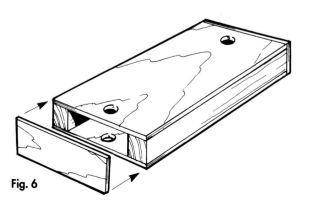

Fig. 6

pencil. Drill the top and bottom together carefully, enlarging the holes to clear the 6 mm (¼ in) dowel. Cut the thinnest pine strip to form front and back, and set the depth of the box to 16 mm (⅝ in) inside. Align it by putting two pieces of dowel in the holes as you glue it together, then glue on the ends (Fig. 6), and, when set, sand the corners neatly. Do not glue the box to the base yet.

3 Using the hole saw, cut all the wheels and the cams and pushrod discs. The sizes are on the pattern page. (I am presuming that this is not the first toy project you are making from this book, so please refer to earlier ones for tips on wheel cutting.)

Two of the small discs are in 6 mm (¼ in) plywood. These are to be the cams, as shown on the patterns. Notch the edge of these to fit the axle and glue them to the inner face of each rear wheel.

The thinner ones are the pushrod discs. Glue these on the ends of two pieces of 6 mm (¼ in) dowel (as in Fig. 7). Note the chamfers on the latter. These are to enable you to fit them on to the figures, which come next.

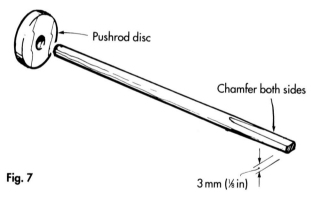

Pushrod disc

Chamfer both sides

Fig. 7

3 mm (⅛ in)

4 Trace off the figure shapes and transfer them to the 3 mm (⅛ in) plywood. Cut the arms and legs at batches of four and the bodies in a pair, for speed and accuracy. Glue the arms and legs on and check the overlap positions by laying them over the pattern page. (Put some polythene over the page to avoid getting glue on the book.)

5 When the figures are dry, finish and paint all the parts, except the pushrods and their discs and the axles. Keep paint away from inside the holes and the ends of the axle bars. Do not paint the bottom of the box, or where it sits on the base.

6 Glue one wheel to each axle; thread the latter through the axle bars – the rear one has the cams, of course. Glue on the other wheels, making sure that the cams are set at 180 degrees to each other (see Fig. 4). Spin to test freedom. Thread the pushrods through the box from the bottom, and measure its position carefully, so that the discs do not rub on the cut-out or the wheels themselves. Mark the position, then glue it to the base. Spin the rear wheels to test for smooth action, and adjust if necessary before the glue sets.

7 Scrape off any paint that has run over the inside of the figures' hands, feet and knees. Glue the figures to the pushrods (as shown in Fig. 8). You will have to prise the knees apart a little, but if the legs are well glued to the body, they will not come off. Turn the wheels until each pushrod is fully down, then slide the figure down until it almost touches the box; also adjust them so that they never get entangled with each other. Then glue them to their pushrods, which you now paint. If you find that the figures occasionally stick in the raised position, sprinkle some talcum powder around the pushrods where they meet the box. This will work its way inside and lubricate the action. *Never, never* use oil on wooden bearings.

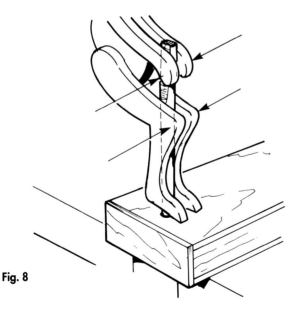

Fig. 8

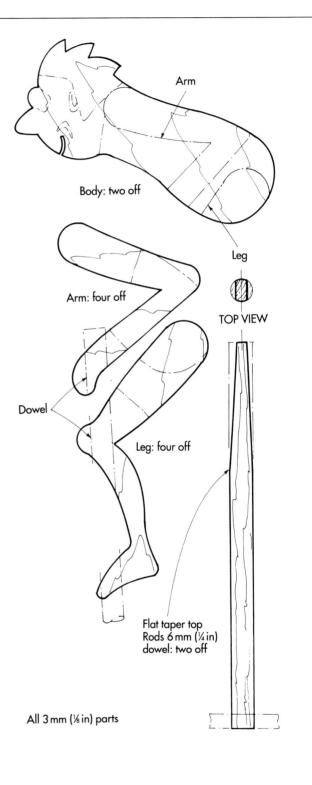

Arm

Body: two off

Leg

Arm: four off

TOP VIEW

Dowel

Leg: four off

Flat taper top
Rods 6 mm (¼ in)
dowel: two off

All 3 mm (⅛ in) parts

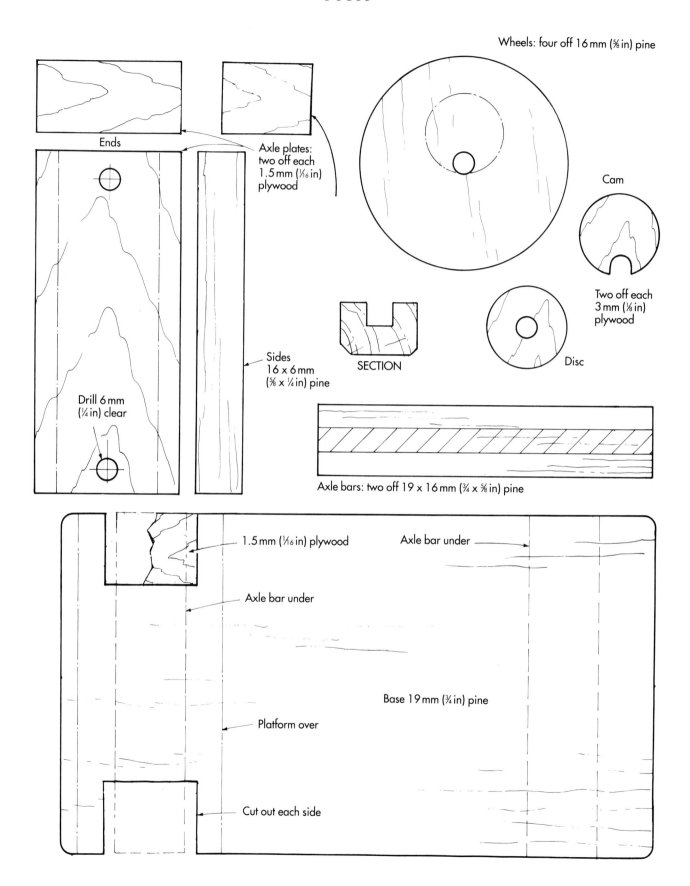

Ends

Axle plates:
two off each
1.5 mm (1/16 in)
plywood

Wheels: four off 16 mm (5/8 in) pine

Cam

Two off each
3 mm (1/8 in)
plywood

Disc

SECTION

Sides
16 x 6 mm
(5/8 x 1/4 in) pine

Drill 6 mm
(1/4 in) clear

Axle bars: two off 19 x 16 mm (3/4 x 5/8 in) pine

1.5 mm (1/16 in) plywood

Axle bar under

Axle bar under

Platform over

Base 19 mm (3/4 in) pine

Cut out each side

TIP

Short dowels – fixing

Some components pivot on short dowels. An arm, for example, has a pivot which passes through the body, before being glued on to the other arm. If the dowel does not go in straight, the action will be stiff, or crocked. The diagram shows a sequence for better fitting. First measure the length of dowel needed, allowing for what goes into each piece, plus the clearance. Mark the distance but leave over-long, to gain accuracy at the next stage.

Now, drill a vertical hole to fit the dowel snugly in a wood block that is a perfectly square cube. Rub the top surface around the hole with candle wax; smooth it level. Glue the dowel into the arm, say, and push the dowel into the hole in the block. When the arm is flat on the waxed surface, the dowel will be in place accurately. Allow it to set. The wax will prevent it sticking to the block.

Finally, sand the top end of the dowel flush, take off the block, and shorten the other end to the mark you made. It is now ready to pass through the body and dry-fit to the other arm for a test, before you paint the toy.

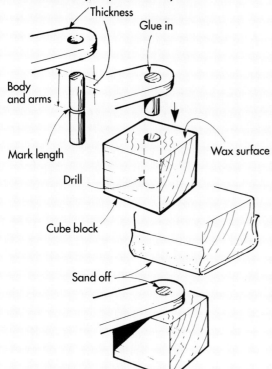

Thickness

Glue in

Body and arms

Mark length

Drill

Cube block

Sand off

Wax surface

TIP

Safety screw locking

Itchy fingers will always find something to undo. The woodscrews in some toys need to be held firmly in place and rendered unscrewable. The sequence for screws upon which parts pivot is shown in the diagram. Fast epoxy is used to lock the screw into the main part of the toy, but it must not get on the moving part or clog its otherwise free hole.

First rub the back of the joint with candle wax to prevent excess glue sticking there.

Push the screw in quite dry and turn it, point downwards, over the hole from which you unscrewed it after testing the toy.

Put a small dab of fast epoxy on its tip and insert it into the hole, without smudging the epoxy around the joint face. Screw it in until the required amount of freedom is reached.

Clean any paint from the slot or cross hole in the screwhead and fill it flush with either neat fast epoxy, or some epoxy mixed with fine sawdust taken from the dust bag of the sanding tool. This will prevent a screwdriver being used by some more experimental young member of the family. If you then smooth it neatly and paint the screwhead, it will look like a neat riveting job.

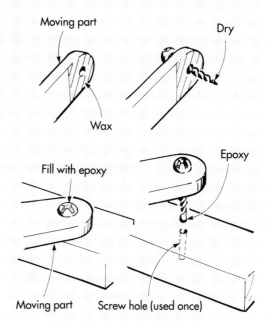

Moving part

Dry

Wax

Fill with epoxy

Epoxy

Moving part

Screw hole (used once)

THE CLEANER

This cleaning lady on wheels never seems to finish scrubbing the floor of her trolley. Like many of the pull-along toys in these projects, an eccentric on the rear axle provides the action. I favour this method because, unlike toys with eccentric wheels, the whole toy does not have to gallop along. An alternative method would have been to have put a screw in one of the wheels, and taken a wire linkage from this.

However, such details are unacceptable for a toy that may be handled by various age-groups, besides it does not look good, and it may get damaged. Eccentrics can be inside or partly hidden, giving an air of mystery, and protecting them from prying fingers. As you will see from Fig. 1, there is nothing mysterious about making eccentrics. In these cases, they are nothing more than a disc of plywood with a groove filed in the edge. The link is a piece of wire wrapped around it.

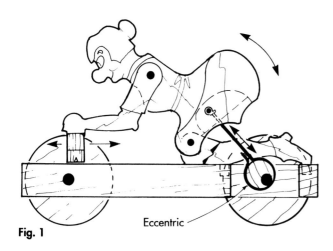

Fig. 1

Eccentric

MATERIALS

3 mm (⅛ in) birch plywood:
  75 x 51 mm (3 x 2 in)
5 mm (³⁄₁₆ in) plywood:
  152 x 127 mm (6 x 5 in)
9 mm (⅜ in) plywood:
  57 x 19 mm (2¼ x ¾ in)
72 x 19 mm (2¾ x ¾ in) pine:
  356 mm (14 in)
3 mm (⅛ in) dowel: 51 mm (2 in)
6 mm (¼ in) dowel: 204 mm (8 in)
1 mm (16 swg) wire
Small screw eye
Carpet thread
String
PVA glue
Epoxy glue
Paint, varnish

TOOLS

Fretsaw
Coping saw (or
  hole saw)
Tenon-saw
Chisel
Drill
Mouse-tail file
Snipe-nose pliers
Sandpaper
Paintbrushes
Rule
Try-square
Pencil
Compass
Carbon paper

1 Using carbon paper and a hard pencil or ball point, trace the patterns of the figure from page 66 on to plywood. Be sure to chose good-quality birch plywood for the legs, as these have to carry the bearings for the knees; if inferior material is used, they will be subject to wear, or may break up while cutting them.

You can cut the inner and outer leg and body pieces, and the arms as pairs, by roughing out areas of ply and pinning them together with short panel-pins. Do not let the panel-pin points protrude below. Thus, you need only to trace down one of each of these parts before pinning. Drill all holes before cutting out the parts. This avoids splitting the grain where holes are near a cut edge, and it ensures that when parts are assembled, the holes are in the right place. These holes also serve to register the laminated pieces, because you can push a dowel of the appropriate diameter through, then withdraw it once the job is clamped together.

When all the pieces are fretsawn, trim any whiskers from the edges, but do not round them. Glue them together, aligned as just described, then clamp them and take out the dowels before the glue starts to set.

2 With compasses, mark out the wheels on one end of the pine strip. You will find that they can be staggered (as in Fig. 2) to leave enough wood to make the base.

Now, the making of wheels may seem daunting if you do not have a lathe. However, small ones like these present no problem if you have an electric drill and a hole saw. There are many wheels in the later projects, and this toy is a good subject on which to practise. You can use a coping saw or a fretsaw to do the same job, but the hole saw, used correctly is much quicker. Suppose you want to do it this way: select the right size of blade in the hole saw, then, when you mark out the wood, allow a few millimetres (just under ⅛ in) for the thickness of the blade; otherwise there will be a flat on the wheel where one overlaps the other, or the edge of the wood!

Drill a 1.5 mm (¹⁄₁₆ in) pilot hole where the compass point has marked. This will serve to guide the 6 mm (¼ in) drill which not only forms the centre of the hole saw, but leaves you with a ready drilled hole for the axle dowel. There is more about wheel making by this method in the tip on page 55.

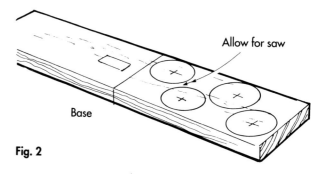

Allow for saw

Base

Fig. 2

The important thing to remember in wheel making is to get the hole straight and the edge truly at right angles to the face of the wood. So if you use a coping saw, a hand fretsaw or a hole saw, keep the blade vertical and the job horizontal. If you have a bench stand for your electric drill, this will be no problem; otherwise, align the tool up by eye, with the edge of a window-frame or a try-square. Go half-way through, then turn the job over and complete it from the other side. This halves the errors.

Right, by some means you now have a set of wobble-free wheels. Turn to the base.

3 Using a tenon-saw, cut the ends of the remaining piece of 72 x 19 mm (2¾ x ¾ in) pine to length for the base of the toy. Then, with drill and chisel, cut a hole for the eccentric, as shown on the pattern page. Work from both sides with the chisel, once the holes are drilled (see Fig. 3). This will make it easier to get the sides vertical.

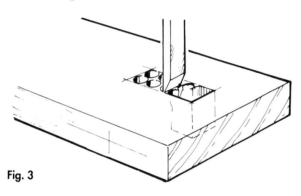

Fig. 3

4 How are you at drilling deep vertical holes? The axles of some of these projects pass right through the solid base, so they must come out in the right place. Of course, the bench stand for the drill is a big help, but no good if the job is not vertical too. Use a perfectly square block of wood, clamped to the side of the base piece to steady it (as in Fig. 4).

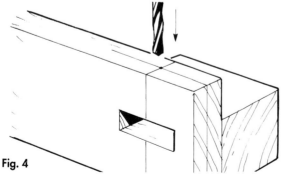

Fig. 4

If you mark the hole centre accurately on both edges of the wood, you can re-position the square support block and turn the thing over to attack it

from the other side. This way, you only have to drill half the depth, thus halving the chances of error.

5 Cut the axles from the 6 mm (¼ in) dowel. Make sure that the wood is truly round, by rolling it in a sloping surface. Sand it, if it is not, and try it in the axle hole. Notice that the drill for this was a clearance size – that is to say, the dowel should spin freely, but not wobble about. The holes in the wheels should be a tight fit to the dowel, and the wheels should not wobble when the axle is spun. Test all the wheels on their axles, but do not glue any yet.

6 Mark and cut (with a fretsaw) the eccentric, which is 9 mm (⅜ in) plywood. Then, with a mouse-tail file, form a narrow groove all round the edge, as in Fig. 5. This keeps the eccentric wire away from the edges. Cut a piece of 1 mm (16 swg) wire and wind it round the groove. It will spring away slightly. You can check the exact shape from the pattern page. You now have a linkage.

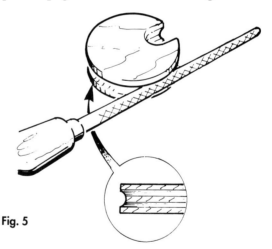

Fig. 5

7 Mark out the brush from the pattern. After smoothing it, glue it to the hands while aligning the shoulders with a small dowel. The body should now be dry, so sand the edges of the laminations to make a smooth outline, but preserve hard edges to the figure.

The legs have lugs to fit into holes in the base, which you drill each side of the slot in the base. Shave the corners of the lugs to make them circular to fit the holes (as in Fig. 6).

All is now ready for sanding, filling and painting, which is best done before final assembly, which we will tackle now.

Fig. 6

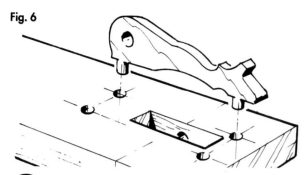

8 Push the axle dowel through the base and press the wheels on. Push the eccentric on the axle so that its notch sits astride it (Fig. 7). Hold it there with a spot of fast epoxy glue, but make sure that it is square to the axle and that the glue does not stick to the base.

When it has set, slide the axle slightly to one side, so that you can insert the wire loop at one side of the eccentric, pull it so that it clipes over the axle, then slide it across and into the groove. It will be very sloppy, so squeeze the loop ends together and wind a piece of carpet thread over the wire joint (as in Fig. 8). Check that when the wheels are turned, the wire moves to and fro smoothly and stays in the groove. Tweak the loop and adjust the thread binding until all is well, then put a spot of epoxy on the thread to hold it. There will be those of you who might make a soldered joint here, but there is no wear here, and little strain.

Fig. 7

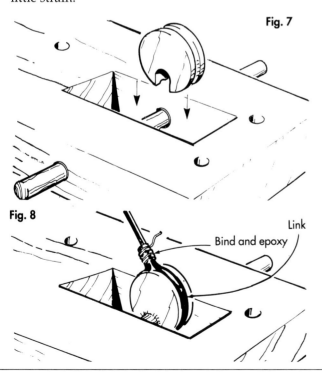

Fig. 8

Link

Bind and epoxy

9 Check that the holes in the legs are a free fit on their dowel at the knees. Adjust with a mouse-tail file if necessary. Glue the leg lugs into their holes in the base, pass the dowel through the figure when in place over the legs (Fig. 9). The dowel should be over length, initially, so that you can withdraw it to make adjustments.

Fig. 9

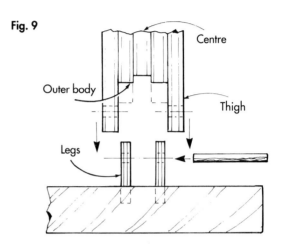

Centre

Outer body

Thigh

Legs

Rock the figure forward and place the wire link in the body, so that it locates with a long panel-pin which you pass through the small hole in the body (Fig. 10). Turn the wheels and the figure should rock. She should come back so that her bottom almost touches her feet. Tweak the wire into a kink to shorten it, if necessary. Finally, pivot the arms to the shoulder on their dowel, which should be a loose fit in the hole in the body.

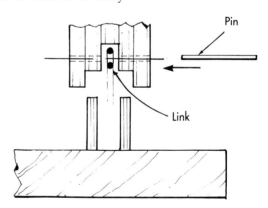

Pin

Link

Fig. 10

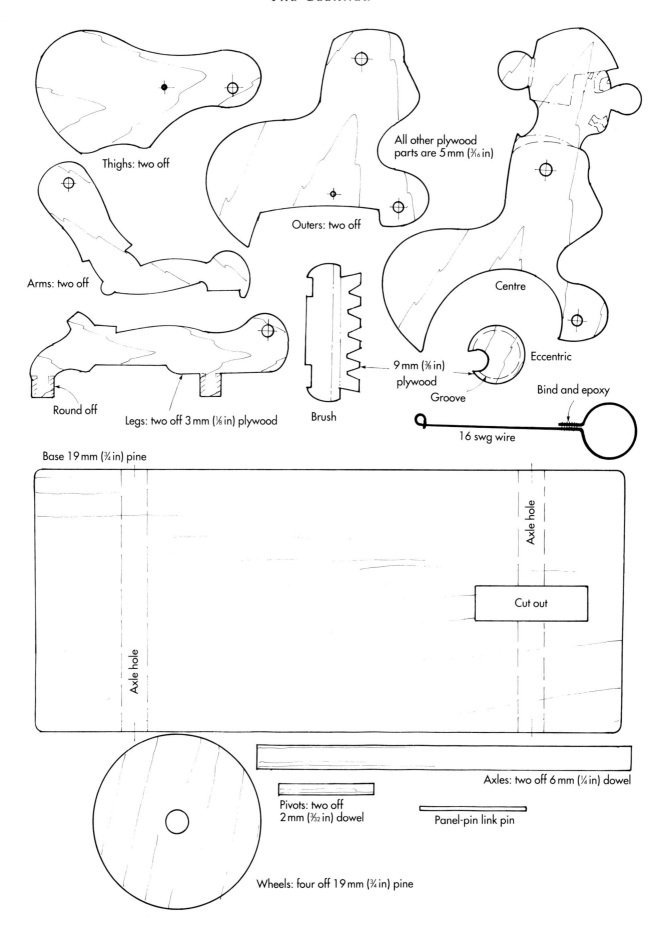

Thighs: two off

Arms: two off

Round off

Legs: two off 3 mm (⅛ in) plywood

Brush

Outers: two off

All other plywood
parts are 5 mm (³⁄₁₆ in)

Centre

9 mm (⅜ in)
plywood

Groove

Eccentric

Bind and epoxy

16 swg wire

Base 19 mm (¾ in) pine

Axle hole

Axle hole

Cut out

Wheels: four off 19 mm (¾ in) pine

Pivots: two off
2 mm (³⁄₃₂ in) dowel

Panel-pin link pin

Axles: two off 6 mm (¼ in) dowel

TIP

Eccentrics

Although eccentrics are described in the projects' construction steps, the following may help you to obtain speedy and accurate results, with what is really an elementary piece of woodwork.

Some eccentrics are small: cut these on a fretsaw; others are large enough to be made with a hole saw. The latter will leave a 6 mm (¼ in) hole in the centre – no matter; it does not affect the working. The pattern pages will show the size; most have the same type of groove around the edge for the wire loop (the Goose is the exception, being smooth).

Axle notch

So, you have cut out the disc. You can use a fretsaw to make a notch to accept the axle. Although the shape is shown on the patterns, remember that the depth of the notch has to be the diameter of the axle *plus* the depth of a groove that goes around the edge. If you make it just to fix the axle, the wire will rub where the groove is interrupted. It is unwise to file the axle to clear it, because it will be weakened.

Fig. 1 shows the notch being made. The rat-tail file, which you may have to use to finish off and true up, should be no more than the diameter of the axle. It will then be useful for freeing up tight axle bearings as well. Support the eccentric in a vice and file downwards to deepen the notch. Keep testing with a piece of dowel, to avoid making it a sloppy fit, for this will result in a poor glue joint and perhaps misalignment as well.

Edge groove

The groove for the wire needs to be around the centre of the edge and of even depth. This is not by any means technical, or engineering in wood. It just works more smoothly if it is evenly done. Fig. 2 shows how to do it.

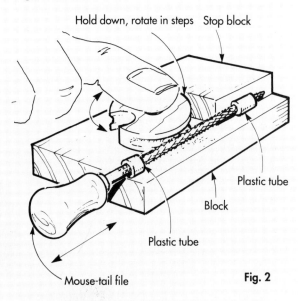

Hold down, rotate in steps Stop block
Plastic tube
Block
Plastic tube
Mouse-tail file

Fig. 2

Make up the simple jig. Two pieces of wood locate the disc and two spacer pieces of plastic tube, or bindings of masking tape on the mouse-tail file, raise the latter clear of the base. The groove is made half-way up the edge of the disc. The spacer at the tip of the file ensures that the latter does not bite in too deeply; the other controls the height. The rest is up to you – holding the disc still for a few file strokes, then loosening your grip on the file handle while you rotate the disc a little, then repeat until the groove is all around the edge.

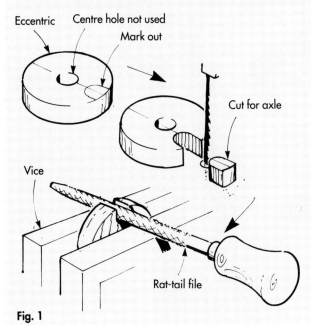

Eccentric Centre hole not used
Mark out
Cut for axle
Vice
Rat-tail file

Fig. 1

BARREL MAN

Push it or pull it, the Barrel Man will run on top of his barrel to keep it spinning. He steadies himself by holding on to the other end of the toy's handle. This is a large toy, because small barrels spin too fast and the little feet of the man would skip too many steps at that speed.

Ideally, the barrel should be turned on a lathe (as was the prototype), but in order to see if you could shape it without one, I made a second, shaping with a chisel, and finishing with a belt sander, mounted on its bench clamp. It should be possible to do without even this, but belt sanders are such conventional tools that I am presuming that you also have one.

The toy works as follows. The figure is mounted so that the legs, which are pivoted on screws, dangle clear of the barrel. There are a pair of large staples driven into the barrel, which, in turn, hit small lugs on the feet, causing them to swing alternately (as shown in Fig. 1). Of course, the action is not mechanically exact, because at some speeds of pushing, the legs get out of step, but this gives a comical, staggering effect, as though the man is missing his footing. Fig. 2 shows the correct angle of the handle. You can set this up to suit the height of the child when you assemble it.

MATERIALS

9 mm (⅜ in) plywood:
    203 x 203 mm (8 x 8 in)
70 x 19 mm (2¾ x ¾ in) pine:
    114 mm (4½ in)
19 x 19 mm (¾ x ¾ in) pine:
    317 mm (12½ in)
76 x 76 mm (3 x 3 in) pine:
    120 mm (4¾ in)
12 mm (½ in) dowel:
    127 mm (5½ in)
Two No. 8 countersunk 25 mm
    (1 in) woodscrews
Two No. 10 countersunk 38 mm
    (1½ in) woodscrews
Two large staples
PVA glue
Fast epoxy glue
Paint

TOOLS

Lathe (optional)
Belt sander
Hand saw
Fretsaw
Chisels
Drill
12 mm (½ in) flat
    bit
File
Screwdriver
Hammer
Sandpaper
Paintbrushes
Pencil
Compass
Rule
Marking gauge
Carbon paper

1 It all starts with the barrel. Mark with the compass on each end of the 76 x 76 mm (3 x 3 in) block, two circles: the outer to represent the maximum diameter; the inner to show the end diameter. Cut away the corners to form an octagon; then again to make 16 faces (as in Fig. 3). You can now take this to the lathe and shape it with the aid of templates shown on page 71. Carve down with your chisel to the end shape. You now have a 16-plank barrel. Each of the flats will be shaped just like a barrel stave before it is finished. You could leave it like this, but the paint would get rubbed off at the 'joints'.

Fig. 3

Once you have followed the lines evenly, all you have to do is shown in Fig. 4. Drill exactly at each end and push a large nail or piece of rod in. Set up the belt sander in its clamp and hold the rods in each hand. With the belt running, lower the barrel at 45 degrees to the belt. It will spin with a scuffing action and round the barrel off evenly. Rock it end to end progressively, until the flats are smoothed to a rounded shape.

You can cut small grooves representing the bands with a marking gauge, then with a file. The ends are flat, but you can hollow these with small chisel strokes – it is not really important to the working of the toy.

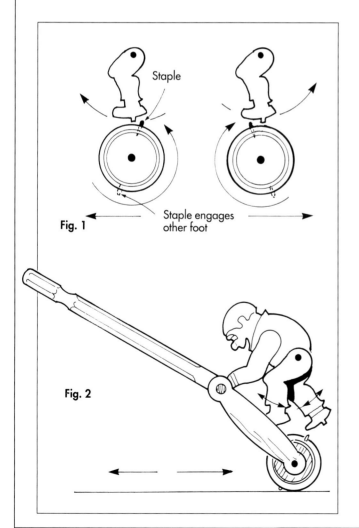

Staple

Staple engages
other foot

Fig. 1

Fig. 2

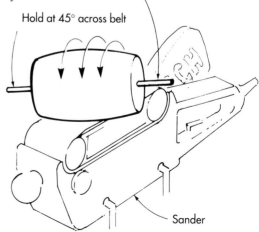

Hold at 45° across belt

Sander

Fig. 4

2 Make the handle from the 19 x 19 mm (¾ x ¾ in) pine, per the pattern page. Drill the hole with the flat bit, with the wood in the vice, to support it against splitting. For the same reason, do this before cutting to length from the hole end. Fig. 5 shows the shaping and surplus length. Take the corners off with a chisel and sand them smooth, but not rounded. File and sand the slight hollow which forms a grip.

3 Cut two rectangles from the 9 mm (⅜ in) plywood to suit the fork pieces, traced down from the pattern. Fix them together temporarily with panel-pins and drill the two end holes (as in Fig. 6). Now cut the outline with the fretsaw as a pair. Mark out and cut the arms and legs in the same way, remembering to drill before sawing.

4 Thread the handle, arms and fork pieces on the 12 mm (½ in) dowel. Apply glue to the ends of the dowel as you add the forks. Do not glue anything else. Rest both forks on a flat board so that they are parallel in both directions and at right angles to the dowel (as in Fig. 7). Allow to set.

5 Trace the body shape on to the 19 mm (¾ in) remaining piece of pine and cut it out on the fretsaw. Prepare all the parts for painting, but do not paint until after the next stages.

6 Measure the distance of the child's hand from the ground, while standing. Apply glue to the dowel at the centre and rotate the handle so that the forks are at 45 degrees to the ground. Slide the figure's hands up to the handle and glue them. Insert the body between the arms, and tilt it. Clip it there with a small clamp. Mount the barrel on the longer screws and pivot the legs on the body, so that their lugs only just clear the barrel. Do all this before the glue sets. Fig. 8 shows the alignment. Make sure that the legs do not hit the arms until they swing well forward. You can make further adjustments by rocking the arms forward and tilting the body.

7 Remove the legs and barrel and paint the toy. Go carefully where the hands meet the handle and the head where it is close to the arms. This is one toy where it would be difficult to glue up after painting. Finally, drive in the staples, so that they protrude about 2 mm (³⁄₃₂ in) from the surface of the barrel, and are under each foot.

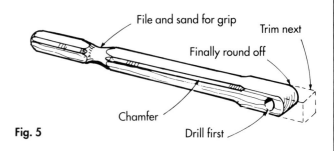

File and sand for grip · Trim next · Finally round off · Chamfer · Drill first

Fig. 5

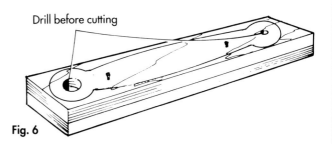

Drill before cutting

Fig. 6

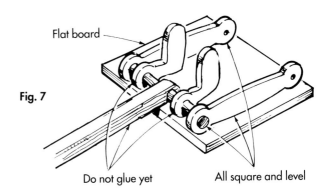

Flat board

Fig. 7

Do not glue yet · All square and level

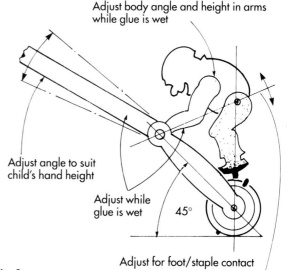

Adjust body angle and height in arms while glue is wet

Adjust angle to suit child's hand height

Adjust while glue is wet · 45°

Adjust for foot/staple contact

Fig. 8

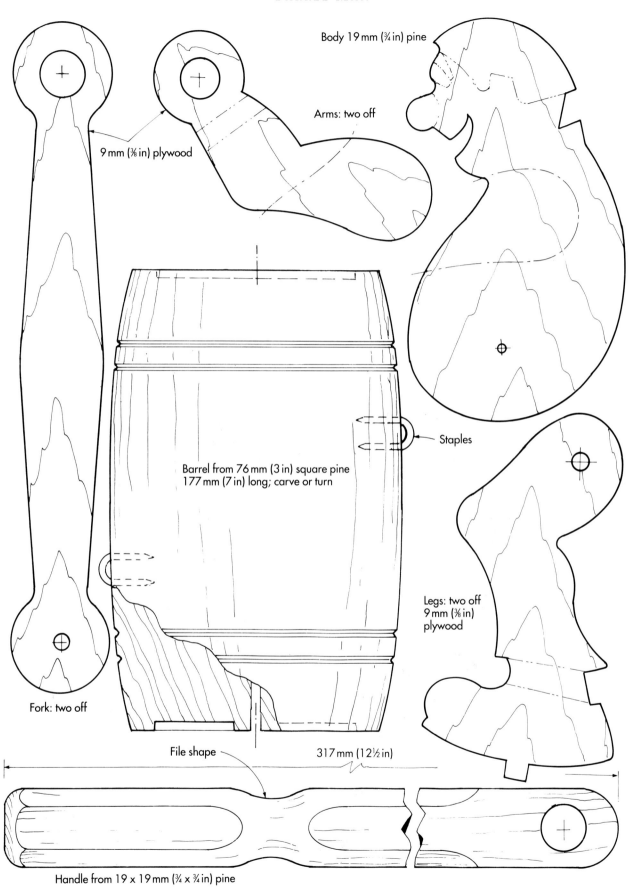

Body 19 mm (¾ in) pine

Arms: two off

9 mm (⅜ in) plywood

Staples

Barrel from 76 mm (3 in) square pine
177 mm (7 in) long; carve or turn

Legs: two off
9 mm (⅜ in)
plywood

Fork: two off

File shape

317 mm (12½ in)

Handle from 19 x 19 mm (¾ x ¾ in) pine

DRUMMER

This pull-along bandsman beats the base drum and taps the cymbal. All the linkage is hidden and, this time, a different type of cam is used. It is a skew plate – seen in Fig. 1, which shows the top view.

The plate is thin and flat, glued at an angle across the rear axle. As the wheels turn, the plate edge moves from side to side. It sits in a forked end of a lever, so that, in turn, swings from side to side. This twists a vertical dowel to swing the body of the bandsman, making drum sticks held in each hand alternately hit the drum and cymbal. A sectioned side view is shown at small scale in Fig. 2.

The construction is simple, even the drum can be made without the aid of a lathe.

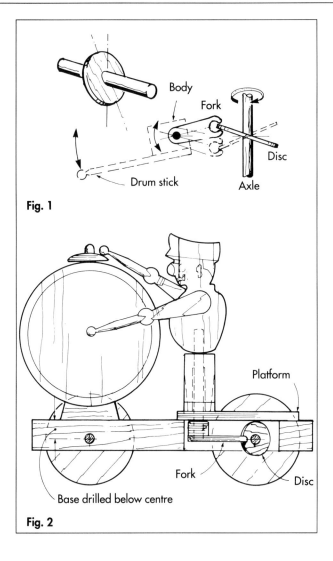

Fig. 1

Fig. 2

1 Start with the base this time. Measure from the template on page 77, and mark out the shape on the 70 x 19 mm (2¾ x ¾ in) pine. Trace the shape of the cut-out and, using the marking gauge, scribe lines on the side edges of the wood to position the axle drilling. Note that these are more than half-way down, so that there is room for the skew plate to clear the top surface (Fig. 2). Mark the top surface.

Drill within the cut-out area to insert the fretsaw blade, and cut it out. The hole will contain the 'works'.

The drilling for the axles must be parallel to the top, so mount the electric drill in its bench stand and clamp a perfectly square block of wood to the base, so that it stands vertically on its side (as in Fig. 3). Drill gently right through if you are confident, or reverse the block and tackle it from the other side, after going half-way. The holes have to clear the 6 mm (¼ in) dowel, which should turn smoothly without wobbling.

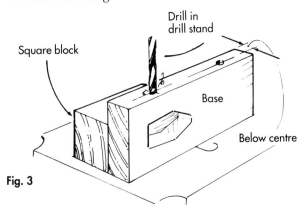

Fig. 3

MATERIALS

3 mm (⅛ in) plywood: 51 x 38 mm
   (2 x 1½ in)
6 mm (¼ in) plywood: 89 x 76 mm
   (3½ x 3 in)
51 x 16 mm (2 x ⅝ in) pine:
   254 mm (10 in)
70 x 19 mm (2¾ x ¾ in) pine:
   190 mm (7½ in)
95 x 19 mm (3¾ x ¾ in) pine:
   190 mm (7½ in)
6 mm (¼ in) dowel: 406 mm
   (16 in)
Two 6 mm (¼ in) washers
PVA glue
Fast epoxy glue
Paint

TOOLS

Tenon-saw
Fretsaw
Drill (preferably
  with stand)
Hole saw
File
Chisels
Glasspaper
Paintbrushes
Pencil
Marking gauge
Carbon paper
Rule

2 Make the drummer's platform from 6 mm (¼ in) plywood. Cut the legs from 19 mm (¾ in) pine and drill it vertically to clear 6 mm (¼ in), while the drill is in its stand.

Round off the feet. Form a shallow groove front and back to give a slight division, but do not get near to the hole, because more drilling has to be done.

Position the feet on the platform and draw round them for reference; mark the front. Holding it there, drill down through the leg hole into the platform. Put a short piece of dowel in that hole for location (as in Fig. 4 overleaf).

Fig. 4

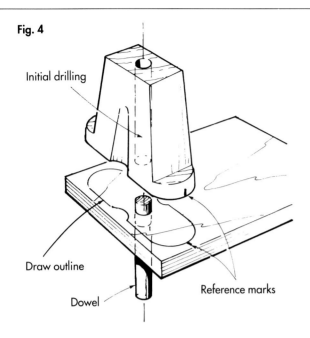

Initial drilling

Draw outline

Dowel

Reference marks

3 In order to reduce friction, the hole in the legs needs opening out more for most of the lower part, leaving the platform to form a bottom bearing. Turn the legs upside-down in the vice and counterbore with a drill the next size up. Put a masking tape flag on it to act as a depth gauge, so that the drill stops 9 mm (⅜ in) short of the top of the legs. See Fig. 5.

Fig. 5

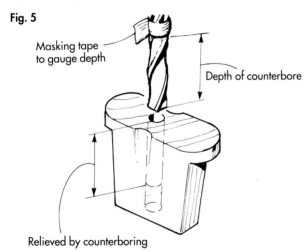

Masking tape to gauge depth

Depth of counterbore

Relieved by counterboring

4 Make the skew disc and fork from really hard 3 mm (⅛ in) plywood. In order to give clearance with small loss of movement, shave the fork as shown in Fig. 6. The hole in the disc will not

Fig. 6

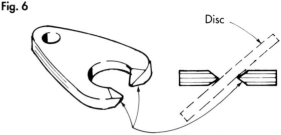

Disc

Chamfer fork to accept disc angle

allow it to lie at an angle, until you file it diagonally with a rat-tail file – aim at about 45 degrees. At this stage you need to set the axle up in position, but for this you should first make the wheels and push them on dry. The wheels are easily cut with the hole saw (as described earlier in other projects). Their size is shown on the template page.

5 Slide the axle, with one wheel pushed on, and a washer, through into the cut-out. Thread on the disc and glue it at the required angle, right at the centre. Use fast epoxy for strength and speed. Push on the other washer and wheel so that they just meet the base.

Cut the 6 mm (¼ in) dowel vertical shaft to length, per the pattern page. Glue the fork on one end and add the spacer to reinforce it. Glue the legs to the platform, pass the dowel through from below, and adjust for free movement before the glue sets. Lower the platform on to the base and slide it about until the fork engages on the disc. Turn the whole thing upside-down to do this. Hold it there and turn the wheels. The fork should swing from side to side smoothly.

If you made the disc the right size and drilled for the axle below centre, there should be clearance. If not, remove the platform and recess it underneath

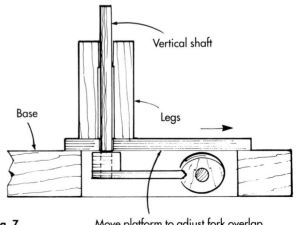

Vertical shaft

Base

Legs

Fig. 7   Move platform to adjust fork overlap

with a chisel, just where the disc rubs. When all is well, glue the platform to the base. Check the action before the glue dries, then pull out the fork and dowel from below, and remove the wheels and washers.

6 Cut out the body and chamfer the corners of the head as shown on the pattern. Cut two identical arms from 6 mm (¼ in) plywood and notch them to fit the drum sticks (Fig. 8). You can shape the sticks in a hand or power drill in the stand, using 6 mm (¼ in) dowel. Hold a piece of folded glasspaper against the side as it spins, to get the taper. Glue the sticks to the arms and the left arm to the body, as shown on the template. Leave the right arm off for now.

7 Cut the drum from the wide pine, using the fretsaw. True up the edge, by finding the centre and mounting it via a thin woodscrew to a board. Then use a sanding block against the edge of the board, while you rotate the drum against it (lathe users can do their own thing).

To get a rim to the drum, you can cut either a pair of thin plywood 1.5 mm (¹⁄₁₆ in) and 3 mm (⅛ in) wide rings and glue them each side, or, do as I did on the prototype: set the marking gauge to 5 mm (³⁄₁₆ in) and run it round the edge of the drum to scribe the flat faces. Go all round gently with a 6 mm (¼ in) chisel to deepen the mark, then shave the faces back to meet the line (Fig. 9). Make the drum stand from the 19 mm (¾ in) pine that is left, per the pattern.

8 Drill the body for its dowel and plug it on dry, after pushing the latter back up through the legs. Glue the drum to its stand, and the stand to the base. Slide the drum back until the centre is in line with the end of the left stick. Let it set there. Make the cymbal from 3 mm (⅛ in) plywood, sanded all around the top edge to form a domed shape. Drill and mount on a stub dowel to the top of the drum. Now glue on the right arm; position it so that its stick tip just wipes the cymbal as the drummer turns left. Adjust the body on the dowel to get a light tap on the drum at full right swing. When the glue is dry, unplug the drummer's body (remember it is on dry), remove the wheels and fork, then sand anywhere that you missed before, and paint all the parts. You will find that there is enough space to reach the drum and legs, when the rest of the parts are out of the way.

Fig. 8

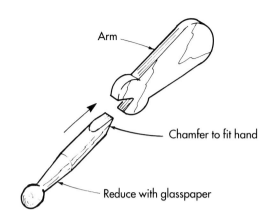

Arm

Chamfer to fit hand

Reduce with glasspaper

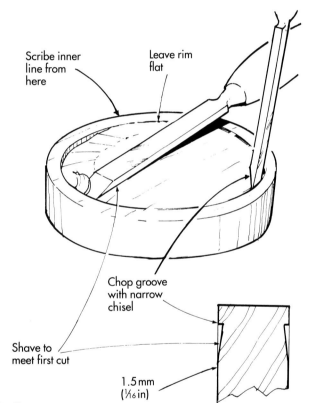

Scribe inner line from here

Leave rim flat

Chop groove with narrow chisel

Shave to meet first cut

1.5mm (¹⁄₁₆ in)

Fig. 9

9 Re-assemble, not forgetting the washers on the rear axle. This time, glue the drummer on to the dowel and re-set his angle to repeat the correct striking positions. As the toy is moved faster, the fork goes a little further, so the drum is hit harder. Fit a screw eye to the front and add string, if you wish. Some children, however, like to push the toys by hand.

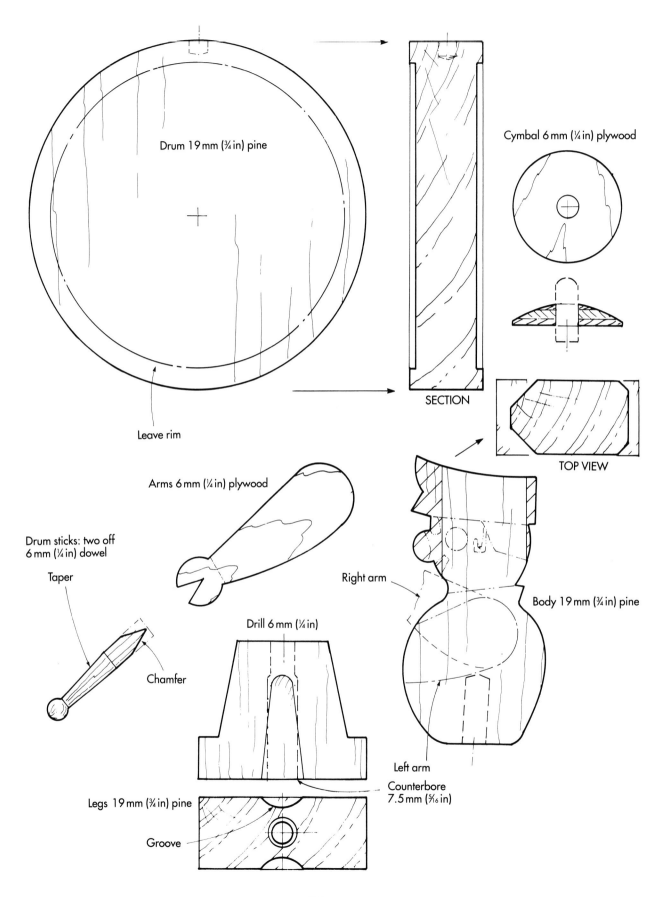

Drum 19 mm (¾ in) pine

Leave rim

SECTION

Cymbal 6 mm (¼ in) plywood

TOP VIEW

Arms 6 mm (¼ in) plywood

Drum sticks: two off
6 mm (¼ in) dowel

Taper

Chamfer

Right arm

Body 19 mm (¾ in) pine

Drill 6 mm (¼ in)

Left arm

Counterbore
7.5 mm (⁵⁄₁₆ in)

Legs 19 mm (¾ in) pine

Groove

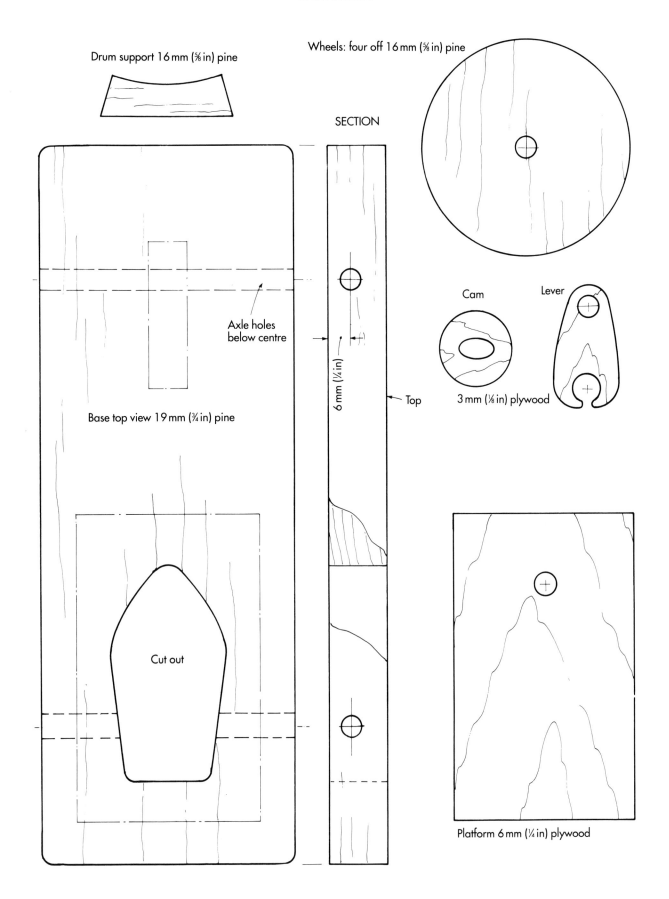

Drum support 16 mm (⅝ in) pine

Wheels: four off 16 mm (⅝ in) pine

SECTION

Axle holes
below centre

6 mm (¼ in)

Top

Base top view 19 mm (¾ in) pine

Cut out

Cam

Lever

3 mm (⅛ in) plywood

Platform 6 mm (¼ in) plywood

SEE-SAW

Smooth, simple action is seen in the pull-along see-saw. It is
another easy, eccentric-driven toy. The linkage is shown in Fig. 1,
transferring rotary to rocking via a wire link. All the works are
hidden inside, between a two-piece base, which can be unscrewed
for adjustments in the course of building – or later, to extract cake
crumbs and treacle!

Fig. 2 shows the side view-cum-section. The figures are cut integral
with the see-saw beam, and the axles run in grooves at the joint of
the two-piece base.

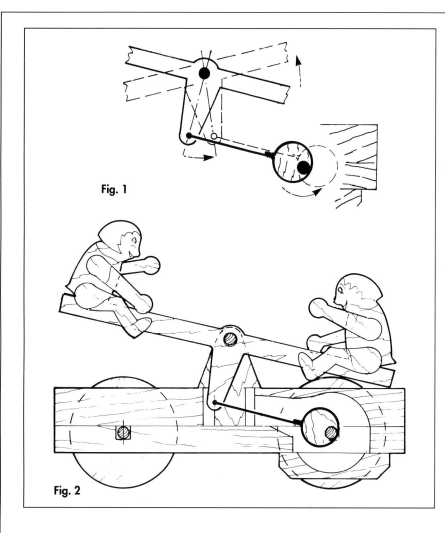

Fig. 1

Fig. 2

MATERIALS

3 mm (⅛ in) plywood: 76 x 51 mm
   (3 x 2 in)
9 mm (⅜ in) plywood: 190 x 88 mm
   (7½ x 3½ in)
70 x 16 mm (2¾ x ⅝ in) pine:
   533 mm (21 in)
70 x 19 mm (2¾ x ¾ in) pine:
   191 mm (7½ in)
6 mm (¼ in) dowel: 254 mm
   (10 in)
1.5 mm (¹⁄₁₆ in) steel wire: 177 mm
   (7 in)
Four No. 8 countersunk 25 mm
   (1 in) woodscrews
Flower wire
PVA glue
Fast epoxy glue
Paint

TOOLS

Tenon-saw
Fretsaw
Chisel
Drill
Hole saw
Mouse-tail file
Screwdriver
Snipe-nose pliers
Sandpaper
Pencil
Paintbrushes
Carbon paper

1 Mark out the base pieces from the templates on pages 82–3. Include the areas that you have to shape to clear the works. For example, Fig. 3 is an underside view of the top base piece. When you use a chisel to cut the shaped recess for the eccentric and link, keep checking to see that the chisel does not break right through the thin area. Keep measuring with a piece of card cut to the right depth, after marking it from the pattern page. The through hole is to take the see-saw brackets.

2 On the lower base piece, make grooves with the tenon-saw for the axles. Drill and carve the cut-out, which has to clear the eccentric and part of the link, but a third piece of thinner wood forms a hollowed-out cover under this. It will be glued on

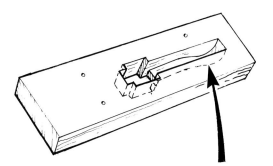

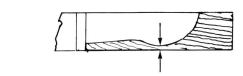

Fig. 3

later. Shape the inside first, while you can clamp it in a vice or Workmate. Then, just take the corners off with a chisel – carve the outside down more to neaten it once it is glued on.

3 Use the templates to select the size of blade in your hole saw, then cut out the wheels and the eccentric with it. If your saw does not have a small enough blade for this one, use a compass and draw it out for cutting on the fretsaw. Form the groove around its rim with a mouse-tail file. If you bind masking tape round each end of the file, and work with the disc near the end of the bench, the tape will act as a height gauge to centre the groove. See the tip on page 67 for a sure way of doing it.

4 Wrap the wire around the groove and take it to the pattern page. Using the pliers, form the rest of the wire to the angles and length shown. The wire will spring open a little, so that you can slip the eccentric out and glue it in the centre of the rear dowel axle, which you cut to the length shown. Fast epoxy is good here – it is strong and lets you press on with the work quicker.

Fig. 4 shows how you replace the wire link and bind the loose end to stop it opening again. Use more epoxy here, but keep it off the wood. A tiny smear of boot polish stops it sticking where it shouldn't. Also glue the wheels on to the axles.

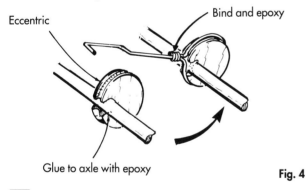

Fig. 4

5 Mark out, drill, then cut out the see-saw brackets and glue them into the hole in the top of the base (Fig. 5). Check with a dowel that the holes are aligned. Now mark out, drill and cut the see-saw with integral bodies. The hole has to be a free fit on the dowel. The small hole is for the wire link end. Then, you need to shave a little off the side to allow the wire to clear the bracket in that side. The tip of the wire must not protrude into the other bracket (see Fig. 6).

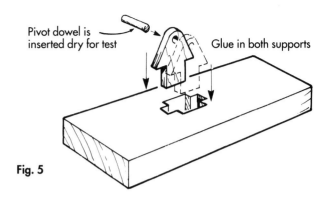

Fig. 5

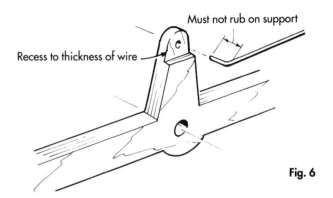

Fig. 6

6 Copy the arms and legs of the children from the pattern page and cut them in pairs from the 3 mm (⅛ in) plywood. Sand them well before gluing them, as shown, to the bodies. The feet must not hang low, or they will hit the base.

7 Place the two base pieces together and mark the position of the rear axle groove from the bottom piece on to the top piece each side. Draw pencil lines across after parting the base pieces. You now know where the axle will be when adjusting the wire link.

Put four panel-pins in to position the axle. Now, with the assembly upside-down, put the see-saw between the brackets without its dowel. Put the link wire in its hole, push the dowel through the brackets and see-saw, then drop the axle between the panel-pins.

Turn the wheels and watch the see-saw rock. If one end hits the base hard, bend the wire kink to lengthen or shorten the linkage (as explained in Fig. 7). You can now remove the see-saw by withdrawing the dowel, and drop the axle out. Pull out the pins and finish off for painting in separate sections.

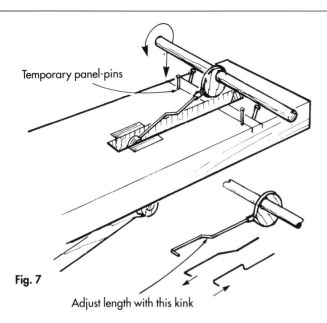

Temporary panel-pins

Fig. 7

Adjust length with this kink

8 After painting, clean away where screws have to go (these are countersunk). Re-assemble everything (Fig. 8) and check that linkage again, in case you put it together the other way round. Finally, spot glue the see-saw dowel to both brackets. This strengthens the brackets too.

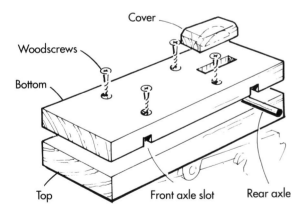

Cover

Woodscrews

Bottom

Top Front axle slot Rear axle

Fig. 8

Shaping
Most of the pine bases of the pull-along toys need to have clearance holes for the drive components. Many are rectangular. You will find that in addition to those that you can cut out on the fretsaw or scroll-saw, or even with a coping-saw, some need a different approach.

Through holes
You may prefer to drill holes, then remove the waste with a chisel. In this case follow the diagram below, which shows the type of grip to use. The left hand rests on the job, and the thumb and two fingers steady the blade, so that it starts on the line that you marked, then continues vertically. Exert pressure downwards with the right hand and thumb and allow the blade to slide. You can introduce a sideways rocking movement to slice, by moving the right hand across.

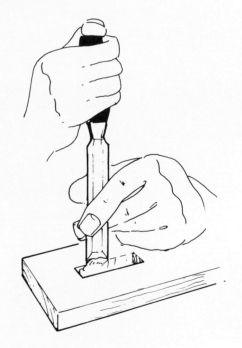

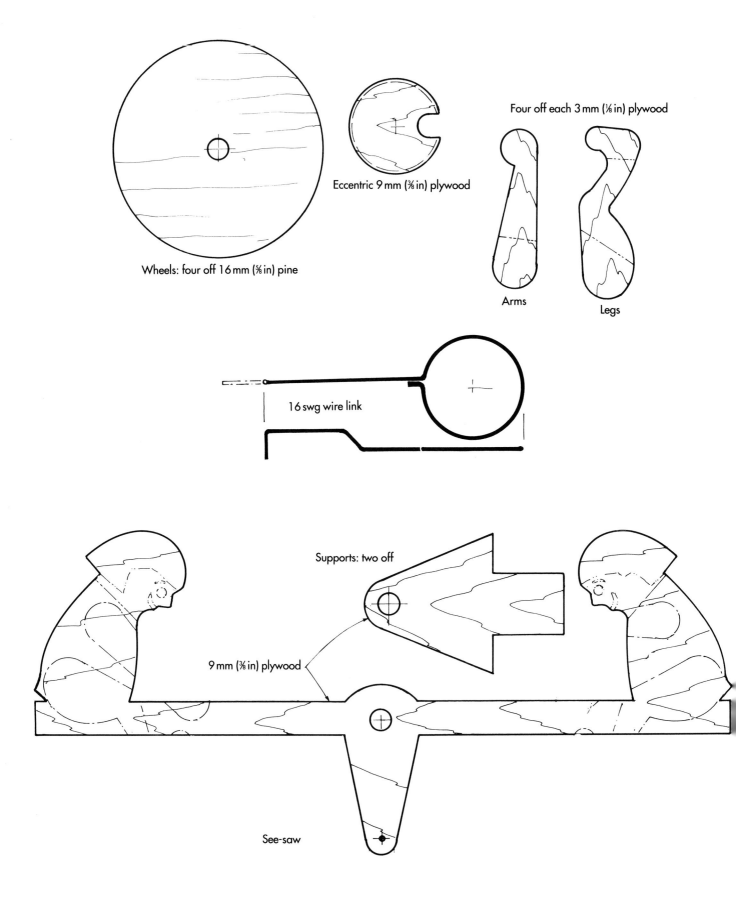

Wheels: four off 16 mm (⅝ in) pine

Eccentric 9 mm (⅜ in) plywood

Four off each 3 mm (⅛ in) plywood

Arms

Legs

16 swg wire link

Supports: two off

9 mm (⅜ in) plywood

See-saw

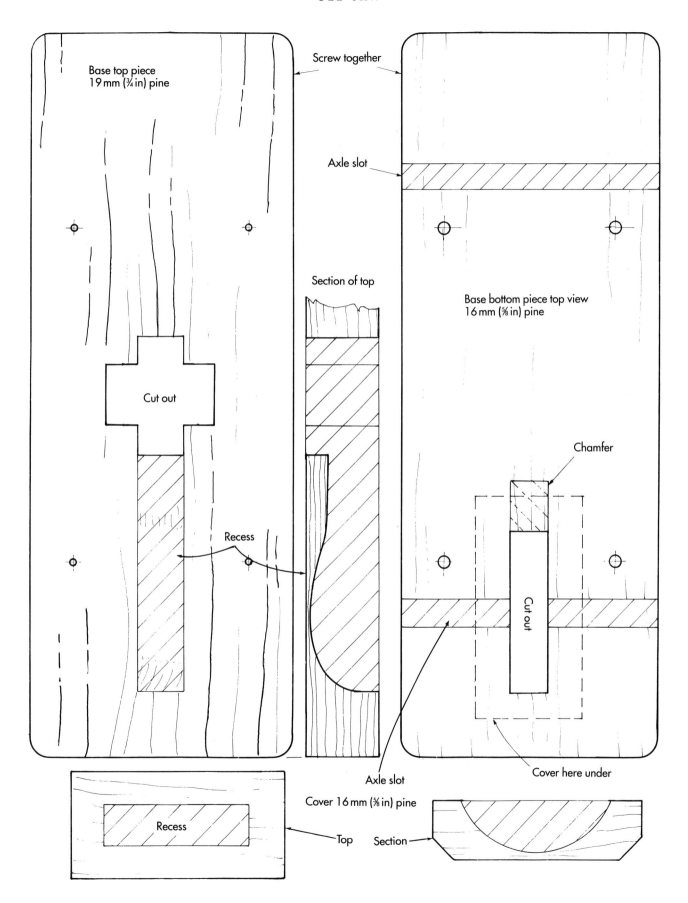

Screw together

Base top piece
19 mm (¾ in) pine

Axle slot

Base bottom piece top view
16 mm (⅝ in) pine

Section of top

Cut out

Recess

Chamfer

Cut out

Axle slot

Cover here under

Recess

Cover 16 mm (⅝ in) pine

Top

Section

WALKING BOOTS

As push-along toys go, this is quite large, because in order to have a realistic stride, each of grandad's old boots needs a large wheel hiding inside. Initial experiments showed that small wheels turn too fast, and they would cause the boots to rattle rather than walk, when pushed or pulled at a child's walking pace. The action is demonstrated in Fig. 1. A close-spaced pair of wheels have their axle on the end of the stick. A bolt in each near the rim is the only connection it has to a hollow boot. The bolts are at 180 degrees to each other. This causes the toe of each boot to lift as it moves forward, drop to the ground and remain almost still as the other boot makes a step forward in the same manner. The heels run on small wheels, to give a shuffling, pedalling type of step.

The inner face of each boot has a cut-out to clear the axle and the interesting path of the wheel, relative to the boot, is shown in Fig. 2, which also shows the construction. Fig. 3 is a cross section to show how the clearance is achieved. There is nothing difficult in the making of this toy – all the experimentation was done before the toy was made, as described.

MATERIALS

4 mm (³⁄₁₆ in) plywood:
    457 x 267 mm (18 x 10½ in)
9 mm (⅜ in) plywood:
    76 x 25 mm (3 x 1 in)
89 x 16 mm (3½ x ⅝ in) pine:
    177 mm (7 in)
95 x 19 mm (3¾ x ¾ in) pine:
    152 mm (6 in)
6 mm (¼ in) dowel: 127 mm (5 in)

12 mm (½ in) dowel: 532 mm
    (21 in)
Two pan-head or round-head
    5 mm (³⁄₁₆ in) bolts, 29 mm
    (1⅛ in) long
Four thin nuts and washers to suit
PVA glue
Fast epoxy glue
Paint

TOOLS

Fretsw (or
    coping-saw)
Rat-tail file
Drill
Hole saw
Screwdriver
Spanner
Sandpaper
Paintbrushes

Pencil
Carbon paper
Rule

Fig. 1

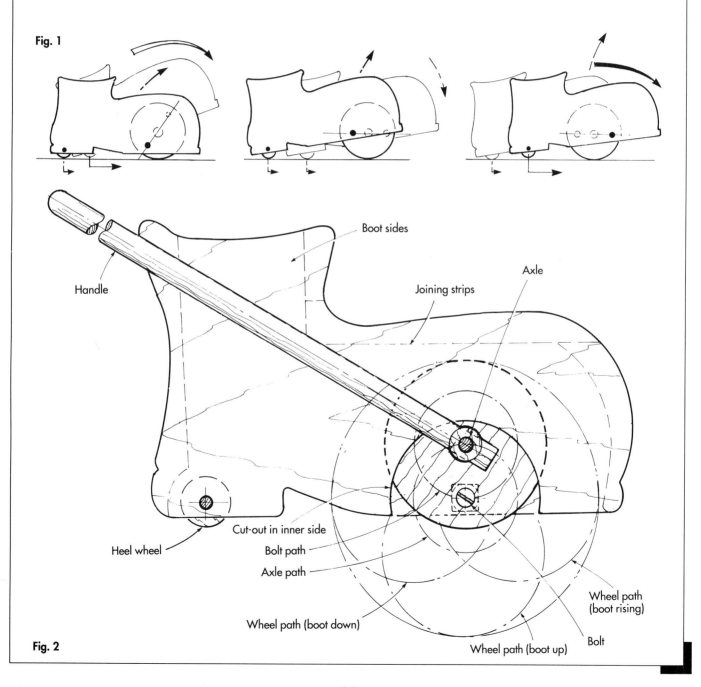

Handle

Boot sides

Joining strips

Axle

Heel wheel

Cut-out in inner side

Bolt path

Axle path

Wheel path (boot down)

Wheel path (boot up)

Wheel path (boot rising)

Bolt

Fig. 2

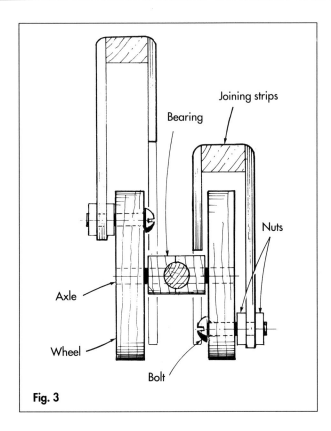

Fig. 3

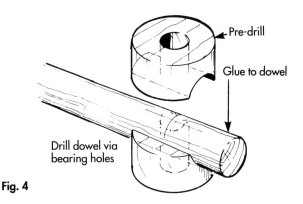

Fig. 4

3 The epoxy on the boot sides should have set, so copy the spacer shapes from the patterns on to the rest of the 95 x 19 mm (3¾ x ¾ in). Check the outer shape against the boot sides, then glue up as shown in Fig. 5. Just check again to see that you have a pair, before clamping to set.

When dry, sand the corners round, so that they do not look so much like boxes, and prepare them for painting, along with the handle/hub.

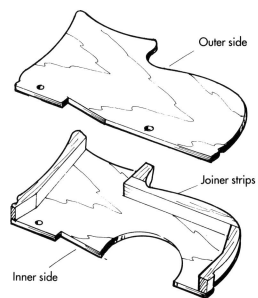

Fig. 5

1 Start with the boot sides. Copy the inner and outer shapes from the patterns on page 88, following the appropriate outlines. Cut the pieces in pairs for accuracy. The bolt holes are important, so drill before cutting, as they are close to the edge. You can reinforce the wood here after drilling, and cutting out, with fast epoxy. Let it soak into the grain by warming the wood with a hair dryer or in the sun. Do not let the glue block the hole. Mark the pieces on the inner faces, so that you do not assemble two left boots!

2 Cut the hub pieces and drill them both together in the centre for the 6 mm (¼ in) axle – clearance size, please. File a hollow in each, to fit exactly half way round the handle dowel, which protrudes past the hub a little for strength. Do not drill the dowel yet, but shape the other hub piece and align it on the dowel with the first. Glue the dowel in. If you scribe a line round the dowel and lengthwise, you can sight it in the hub hole (as shown in Fig. 4). Drill right through when set.

4 With the small hole saw, cut the two heel wheels. You have to fret the spacers as they are so small. Check that they spin easily on the 6 mm (¼ in) dowel. All the parts can now be painted. When hard and dry, go to the last stages.

5 Glue one wheel on to its axle; pass the axle through the bearing and glue the other wheel on. Check for wobble-free movement and that the wheels have their holes at 180 degrees.

Put the bolts through the wheels to point outwards with a washer under the head and on the free end. They should turn smoothly, particularly if you have chosen bolts with threads that stop some way short of the head (as in Fig. 6). Drop one wheel into its boot, fit one nut and push the bolt through the side of the boot. Lock it there with the other nut. The nuts lock to grip the boot, and the bolt should be free in the wheel. Repeat with the other wheel and boot. Check back with Fig. 3 for those clearances. When you are sure that all move freely, but without scraping the sides, put fast epoxy on the nuts to secure them to the wood.

6 Thread the heel axles through the boot side, spacer, wheel, spacer and other side. Glue the spacers to the axle and the axles to the boots, leaving the wheel free (see Fig. 7). The boots draw attention to themselves by their comical action and clattering along the pavement. They can be pushed or pulled, as they swing quite freely until they are lowered to the ground.

The wheels are best painted black or dark grey, so as to escape notice. Keep the boots a bright colour.

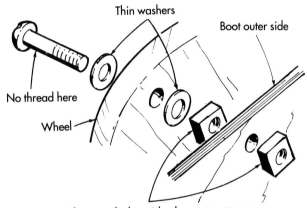

Thin washers

Boot outer side

No thread here

Wheel

Fig. 6   Thin nuts, lock to side, then epoxy to secure

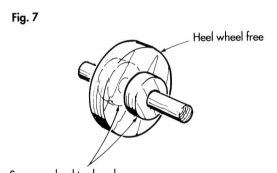

Fig. 7

Heel wheel free

Spacers glued to dowel

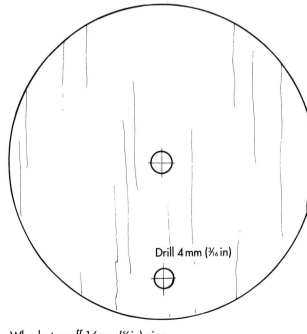

Drill 4 mm (³⁄₁₆ in)

Wheels: two off 16 mm (⅝ in) pine

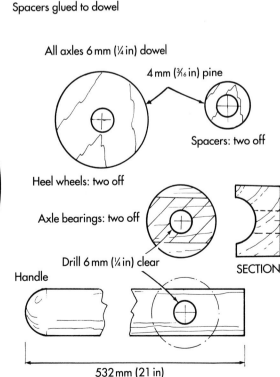

All axles 6 mm (¼ in) dowel

4 mm (³⁄₁₆ in) pine

Spacers: two off

Heel wheels: two off

Axle bearings: two off

Drill 6 mm (¼ in) clear

Handle

SECTION

532 mm (21 in)

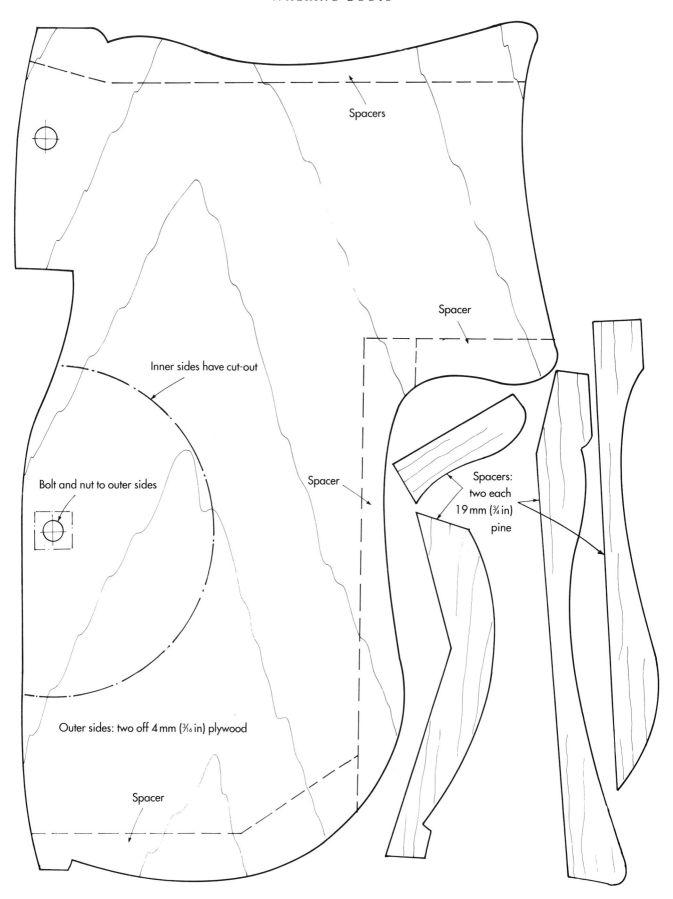

Spacers

Spacer

Inner sides have cut-out

Spacer

Bolt and nut to outer sides

Spacers:
two each
19 mm (¾ in)
pine

Outer sides: two off 4 mm (³⁄₁₆ in) plywood

Spacer

TIP

Forming wire parts

Although this is almost entirely a woodwork book, some simple wire parts are needed on a number of the projects. Most of them are made in comparatively soft iron-galvanized wire sold at hardware shops for garden use. Garden shops usually sell plastic-coated wire.

Three projects use thin springy steel wire. Known as piano wire or music wire, you can buy it from model-making shops.

Here, then, are some tips to help you to get the shapes right – the easy way. If your pliers are strong, but pointed, and with a cutting part, all you need is a metal vice or flat piece of metal and a hammer. The pattern pages show all the bends full size, and you can check the parts on the finished wood components for fit, as you go.

Now, there is no soldering, because the strain on the wire is so small. Where an end has to be secured, you can bind it with thread or flower arranger's wire and glue it with fast epoxy glue. This seals the join and adds strength.

Sharp bends

The most tricky are those near the end of the wire. You have to grip the wire so tightly as you twist it over that the tips of the pliers jaws may slip off or even get distorted. Follow Fig. 1 for the correct sequence.

If you need to see how much short end is to be bent, look at it near the end of the jaws, but do not make the whole bend with it there. If you must bend it at all, give it a small angle; then with something to guide you, slide it further up the jaws, where the grip will be better.

Rest the long part of the wire on a hard, preferably metal surface and press the pliers down on to it hard, as you rotate them to make the bend. Now you have a 90-degree angle, but perhaps it is not as sharp as the pattern shows. Grip the short end in the metal vice, right up to the start of the rounded bend. Tap the exposed part of the bend down with a hammer until the inner part of the bend is sharp.

Use this method for any short bend or kink that has to be very sharp. Remember that it is the long end that is bent over. Then the short part will not be too short.

Loops on eccentrics

Make the short-end bend first. Then, using the more pointed part of the pliers, gently wind the wire in a complete circle until it matches the shape on the pattern page. It is soft enouth to press around a large eccentric groove with the fingers. It will spring apart slightly, but this will help when you need to fit it in place.

Do the test bending with a scrap piece of dowel in the eccentric notch. Aim to get a smooth, easy fit, without the wire sliding off the edge of the groove. It should certainly not be stiff or uneven to turn.

Hold the short bent end against the straight part as it leaves the loop. Adjust the bend of the straight part/loop until you get it right. Do not make the joint until the final assembly, usually after painting the wood parts.

Squeeze the loop with your fingers and wind the thread or flower wire over six or eight times to hold the joint. Apply a small drop of fast epoxy glue to the joint with a matchstick, but keep the glue away from the eccentric itself. If you are working in a confined space, coat the eccentric with wax from a candle, or boot polish. This will prevent the glue sticking where it shouldn't.

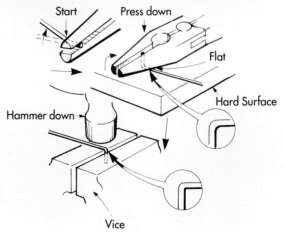

HOBBY-CROC

The traditional hobby-horse is little more than a head on a stick. The end of the stick trails on the ground, and either wears itself out or cuts up the floor covering. This 'horse' is a crocodile. It snaps its jaw by means of an eccentric on a pair of wheels that protect the floor. The stick is long, so that the wheels are well clear of the child's feet. A thin wire pulls the jaw up, and its own weight allows it to drop. The wire runs in a piece of hollow curtain spring, which is fixed in a groove in the stick, so as not to get in the way. Fig. 1 shows the linkage. The sectional details appear in Fig. 2, which has been foreshortened to fit the page.

There is not much woodwork in this simple, if large, toy. Your artistic skill may provide you with variants. This, and the next toy, both use the same eccentric and linkage details.

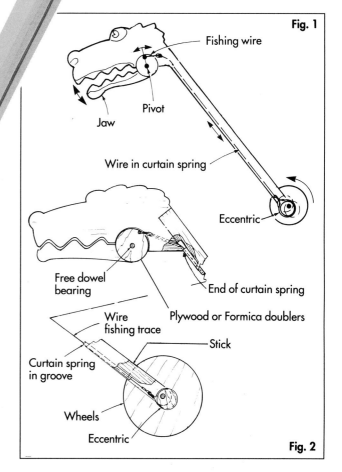

Fig. 1

Fishing wire

Pivot

Jaw

Wire in curtain spring

Eccentric

Free dowel bearing

End of curtain spring

Plywood or Formica doublers

Wire fishing trace

Stick

Curtain spring in groove

Wheels

Eccentric

Fig. 2

MATERIALS

0.8 mm (½₂ in) plywood or
Formica: 76 x 76 mm (3 x 3 in)
6 mm (¼ in) plywood: 114 x 32
mm (4½ x 1¼ in)
95 x 19 mm (3¾ x ¾ in) pine:
533 mm (21 in)
19 x 19 mm (¾ x ¾ in) pine:
622 mm (24½ in)
6 mm (¼ in) dowel: 89 mm (3½ in)
1.5 mm (¹⁄₁₆ in) steel wire: 127 mm
(5 in)
Steel fishing trace (7 lb strain):
660 mm (26 in)
Short piece of thin brass tube (for
crimping above)
Curtain spring wire: 507 mm
(20 in)
One No. 4 12 mm (½ in) round-
head woodscrew
Two No. 8 countersunk 19 mm
(¾ in) woodscrews
PVA glue
Fast epoxy glue
Paint

TOOLS

Fretsaw
Tenon-saw
Chisel
Drill
Hole saw
Screwdriver
Snipe-nose pliers
Sandpaper
Paintbrushes
Pencil
Carbon paper
Rule
Marking gauge

Following Fig. 3, recess the head using a small chisel to remove one third of thickness from one side, to the shape of the jaw hinge. Glue in one disc with fast epoxy. Then, when set, do the same on the opposite side. It will then look like the illustration.

2 Fix the second disc with epoxy. Measure the finished thickness, and saw a slot in the jaw as per the pattern page. The width of the slot has to accommodate the facing discs (Fig. 4). When you have tried the jaw hinge with a piece of 6 mm (¼ in) dowel, fix the last two discs on the outside of the jaw as shown. You now have the opportunity of freeing up the hinge by sanding or scraping the sides of the jaw slot, while the outer discs provide reinforcement.

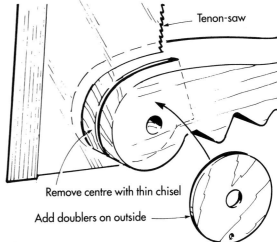

Tenon-saw

Remove centre with thin chisel

Add doublers on outside

Fig. 4

3 Drill a slanting 2 mm (³⁄₃₂ in) hole from the edge of the hinge recess to come out in the rebate that is to fit the stick (Fig. 5). This is to take the cable that lifts the jaw. Open out the ends of the hole with a file to allow the cable easy movement.

1 Trace the head and jaw patterns (from page 93) down on to the 19 mm (¾ in) pine, and cut them out on the fretsaw. Make four facing discs from the thin plywood or Formica. These also reinforce the joint which comes next.

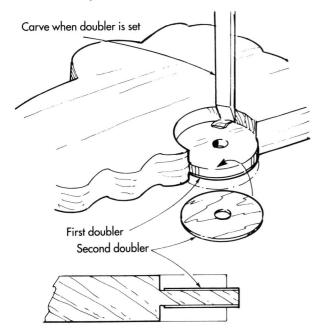

Carve when doubler is set

First doubler

Second doubler

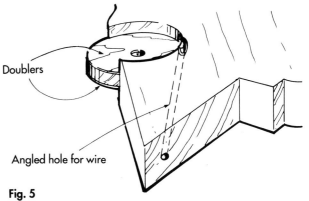

Doublers

Angled hole for wire

Fig. 3   **Fig. 5**

4 Make the wheel bearing from the 6 mm (¼ in) plywood. Use it as a jig to drill the holes in the end of the 19 x 19 mm (¾ x ¾ in) pine stick, which you continue to shape as shown on the pattern page, and in Fig. 6. Use the tenon-saw and chisel to form recesses for the plywood bearing piece and the eccentric, clearance for the wire link, and a groove to house the curtain spring wire. Do not glue the bearing piece on yet.

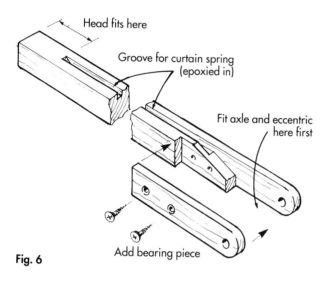

Head fits here

Groove for curtain spring (epoxied in)

Fit axle and eccentric here first

Add bearing piece

Fig. 6

5 Cut the eccentric with the hole saw from 6 mm (¼ in) plywood. You will probably have to tack down this piece to a larger piece in order to secure it for cutting – that is, if you have not opted for cutting it with the fretsaw, or have a larger piece spare.

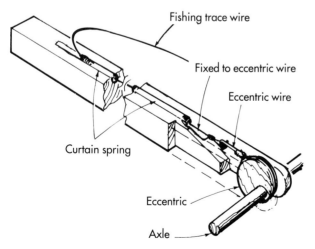

Fishing trace wire

Fixed to eccentric wire

Eccentric wire

Curtain spring

Eccentric

Axle

Fig. 7

File a groove around its edge and fix it in the centre of the 6 mm (¼ in) dowel that is to become the axle. Use fast epoxy.

Form the eccentric wire to the shape on the pattern. Wrap it around the eccentric and bind the end with thread or flower wire, plus a dab of epoxy. Check for smooth movement. Form a small loop in the free end to take the fishing trace. The wire comes off the lower side of the eccentric, as you will see from the underside view in Fig. 7. Glue the curtain wire in the groove and thread the trace through it. Loop the trace through the wire link and crimp it with the brass tube (Fig. 8). Fishing tackle shops sell small crimp tubes with the trace.

You can now glue and screw the bearing piece to the stick. Glue the head on the other end. Thread the trace through the hole drilled from the hinge as you do this. Give it a tweak or two as the glue dries, to keep it free.

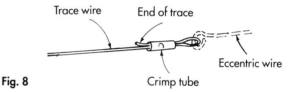

Trace wire

End of trace

Eccentric wire

Crimp tube

Fig. 8

6 Mark out, drill and cut the wheels on the fretsaw. True up the edges as a pair on a scrap of dowel. Paint the whole toy before fitting the wheels or the jaw.

7 Pivot the jaw on its dowel. Make sure it drops loosely and does not stick, due to paint getting on the rubbing faces. Talcum powder acts as a good lubricant for these joints.

Turn the wheels so that the wire is pulled, rather than slack. Close the jaw and put a small screw in the facing disc in line with the trace wire exiting from the hole. Loop the trace round the screw and add a crimp tube.

The jaw should droop a little as the wheels are turned, and close once per turn. Do not have the wire tight, or the wheels will skid. Large, wide rubber bands glued on the wheels help the grip on smooth surfaces. Epoxy the screws to prevent them coming out.

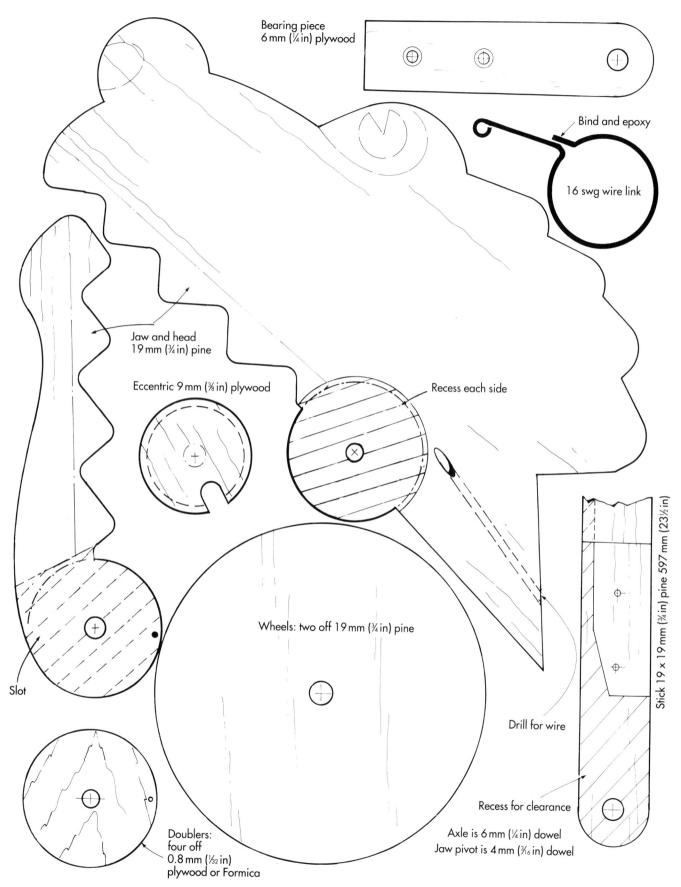

Bearing piece
6 mm (¼ in) plywood

Bind and epoxy

16 swg wire link

Jaw and head
19 mm (¾ in) pine

Eccentric 9 mm (⅜ in) plywood

Recess each side

Wheels: two off 19 mm (¾ in) pine

Slot

Stick 19 x 19 mm (¾ in) pine 597 mm (23½ in)

Drill for wire

Recess for clearance

Axle is 6 mm (¼ in) dowel
Jaw pivot is 4 mm (³⁄₁₆ in) dowel

Doublers:
four off
0.8 mm (¹⁄₃₂ in)
plywood or Formica

FLOPPY EARS

The large plywood ears of this version of the hobby-horse are free
to swing fore and aft, and in fact, do so when the owner gallops
along in a jerky manner. When he or she goes at a steadier pace, the
wheels and eccentric keep them swinging via the identical cable
arrangement that is used on the Hobby-Croc. This toy is a little
easier to make, in that there is no shaping of a hinge. You could
make them both at the same time, while you are in the swing of it.
Fig. 1 shows that the trace that moves the ears is below the pivot in
this toy and it runs in a recess to enter the top end of the curtain
spring described in Hobby-Croc.

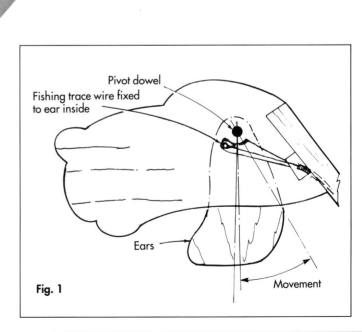

Fig. 1

Pivot dowel

Fishing trace wire fixed
to ear inside

Ears

Movement

MATERIALS

6 mm (¼ in) plywood:
 178 x 152 mm (7 x 6 in)
95 x 19 mm (3¾ x ¾ in) pine:
 533 mm (21 in)
19 x 19 mm (¾ x ¾ in) pine:
 622 mm (24½ in)
6 mm (¼ in) dowel: 101 mm (4 in)
1.5 mm (¹⁄₁₆ in) steel wire: 127 mm
 (5 in)
Steel fishing trace (7 lb strain):
 660 mm (26 in)
Curtain spring wire: 507 mm
 (20 in)
PVA glue
Fast epoxy glue
Paint

TOOLS

Fretsaw
Tenon-saw
Chisel
Drill
Hole saw
Screwdriver
File
Snipe-nose pliers
Glasspaper
Paintbrushes
Pencil
Marking gauge
Carbon paper
Rule

2 Notice the notch in the back of the head where the curtain wire exits (pattern page and in Fig. 3), which also shows the recess carved for the trace wire in the head side. The ears hide most of this when they are in position.

In this toy, the trace is fixed and fed down to the wheel end of the stick. Glue one ear to its pivot dowel. The other will be glued on when the painting is done and the dowel passed through the head.

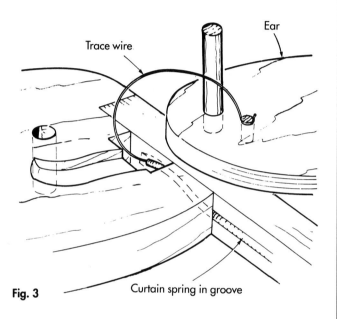

Fig. 3

Trace wire
Ear
Curtain spring in groove

1 Trace the pattern shapes from page 96 to the 19 mm (¾ in) pine for the head and wheels, and on to the 6 mm (¼ in) plywood for the eccentric, bearing piece and ears. Cut them out using the fretsaw. You can do the ears as a pair, including drilling for the 6 mm (¼ in) pivot dowel. The hole in the head for the latter has to be a loose clearance. A smaller hole is needed in one ear, for attaching the trace wire. Secure this by doubling it over a piece of dowel, and driving the latter in from the inner face (as shown in Fig. 2).

3 Make all the rest just as shown in the Hobby-Croc project, but this time make the connection and adjustments at the link wire end instead of at the head.

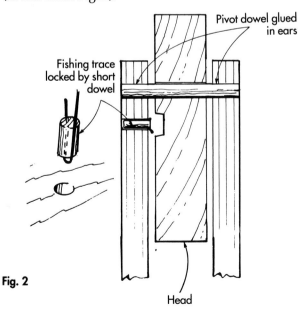

Pivot dowel glued in ears

Fishing trace locked by short dowel

Fig. 2

Head

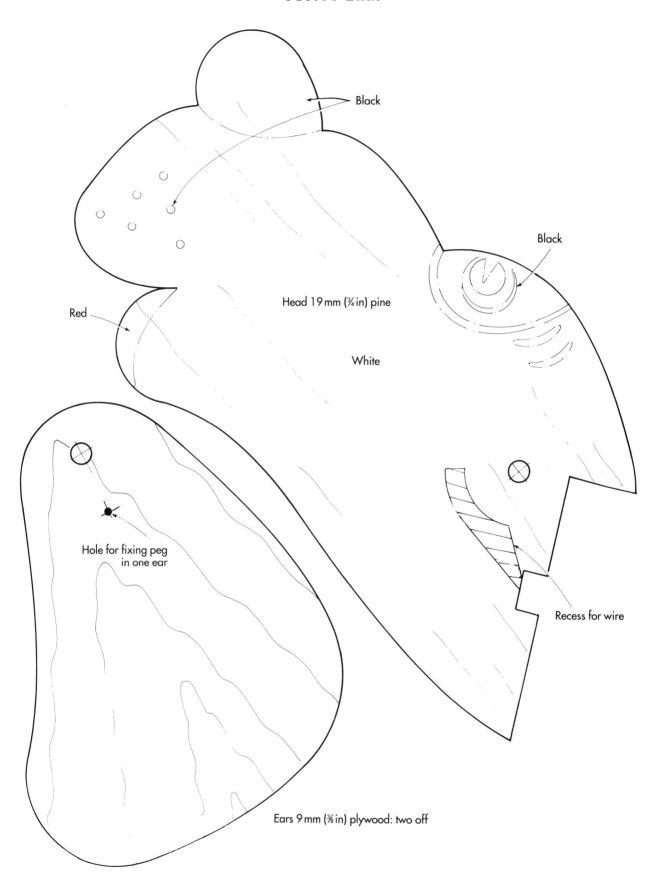

Black

Black

Head 19 mm (¾ in) pine

White

Red

Hole for fixing peg
in one ear

Recess for wire

Ears 9 mm (⅜ in) plywood: two off

TIP

Safety Tips

1 Do not modify the projects; each has been checked to see that there are a minimum of spaces where fingers can be wedged (although, knowing children, they may find some play technique that does this).

2 There are no sharp, spiky points or sharp edges in the original designs, so do not introduce any by failing to sand the edges or leave ends of wire protruding, contrary to design.

3 Do make sure that all screws are firm. It is sometimes possible that the hole which receives the thread of the screw is drilled too large or too deep. The screw is put in with little effort. This should be a signal either to replace the screw with one of the next number up (thicker), or to use fast epoxy on the tip when it is put in finally. Apply this method only after final assembly after painting and testing. There is a tip dealing with secure screws on page 61.

4 Wherever possible, pivots are wooden dowels, glued in place, so do not substitute screws where the design shows dowels.

5 Your choice of project should be influenced by the age of the child. Very small children may only get pleasure from chewing or pulling at parts of the toy. The interactive effect is more suited to those who are inquisitive, without being unconsciously destructive. Individual children vary in the age when a particular toy is suitable, and you may observe the effect of other toys, before making one to suit and encourage your child.

6 Always use non-toxic paint for all stages of the painting, and keep some for touching in scratches later.

TIP

Rebates

A rebate in these projects sometimes has to be more than a rectangular recess. Take the clearance for the drive on Waltzers, for example. This is shaped to a curve at the ends and has a second recess below it. It is not as complicated as words would make out. You will need a coping saw, tenon-saw and chisel. Follow Fig. 1.

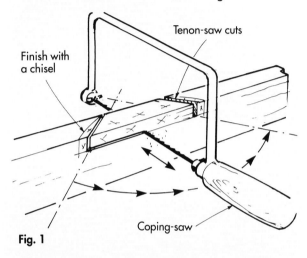

Tenon-saw cuts

Finish with a chisel

Coping-saw

Fig. 1

Make cuts with the tenon-saw at each end at the appropriate angle, near to the curved line. Insert the coping-saw at one cut and saw across on the guide line. Swing the saw round in an arc to finish at the second saw cut. Trim up with a chisel held flat. Then carve down with the chisel to produce a curve each end. These edges are out of sight and will not need more than sandpapering, let alone painting, so a slight slip-up may not spoil the external super finish.

You may, if you wish, make a series of radiating cuts with the tenon-saw, and go straight to the chisel stage (as in Fig. 2).

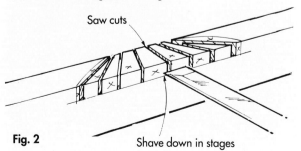

Saw cuts

Fig. 2

Shave down in stages

Soccer Player

This table toy will test strength and aim. When a trigger is thumped down firmly, the soccer play kicks the ball so hard that it goes right back over his head and lands on his bottom. The linkage for this starts almost over centre (as shown in Fig. 1). It has the effect of accelerating the leg rapidly. There is a little resilience in the wire pushrod, and this provides an initial storage of energy as it bends very slightly. The full effect is shown in Fig. 2. When a gentle tap is given to the trigger, the ball only goes part of the way up and swings back again after kicking. The ball is a table-tennis type and it is fixed on a thin piece of music wire, hanging from the soccer player's right wrist. He kicks left-footed, and is shown in side view in Fig. 3, together with a cross-section.

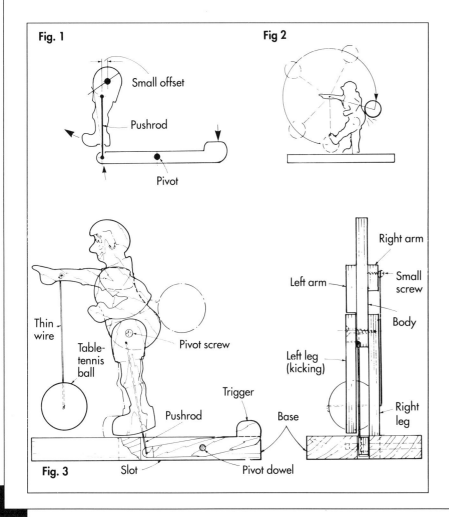

MATERIALS

9 mm (⅜ in) plywood: 229 x 127 mm (9 x 5 in)
95 x 19 mm (3¾ x ¾ in) pine: 191 mm (7½ in)
5 mm (³⁄₁₆ in) dowel: 64 mm (2½ in)
0.8 mm (¹⁄₃₂ in) piano wire: 152 mm (6 in)
1.5 mm (¹⁄₁₆ in) piano wire: 102 mm (4 in)
One table-tennis ball
One No. 4 9 mm (⅜ in) round-head woodscrew
One No.10 countersunk 25 mm (1 in) woodscrew
Small washer
PVA glue
Fast epoxy glue
Paint

TOOLS

Tenon-saw
Fretsaw
Drill
Chisel
Snipe-nose pliers
Screwdriver
Paintbrushes
Glasspaper
Pencil
Carbon paper
Rule

1 Trace down from page 101 and cut out all the 9 mm (⅜ in) plywood parts, using a fretsaw. Recess the body where the inner face of the left leg will go, with a chisel, so that the 1.5 mm (1/16 in) wire will clear (as shown in Fig. 4). Bend the wire sharply where it turns outwards into the left leg. You can check this from Fig. 3 as well.

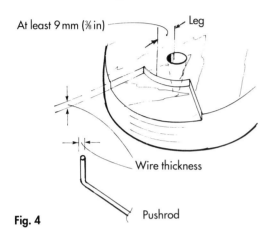

Fig. 4

2 Measure the wire length on the pattern page, and form the second right-angle bend. Both bends can be made sharp, if you clamp the wire in a vice and hammer it flush (as shown in Fig. 5). Check that the wire moves smoothly, but without slop in the holes in the leg and in the trigger, which you also have to notch (as shown in Fig. 5). Avoid this end of the wire rubbing on the base later, by trimming flush any that is protruding.

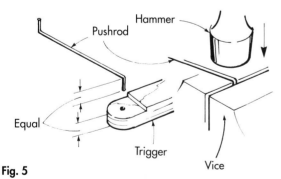

Fig. 5

3 Cut the base from the 95 x 19 (3½ x ¾ in) pine, following the shape on the pattern page. Use the fretsaw to form the rebate for the soccer player's right foot. Continue along to complete the long slot for the trigger. Check the clearance for the trigger in here.

Clamp the base upright on edge and drill part way through, as shown on the pattern and in the section in Fig. 3. This is for neatness. The pivot dowel for the trigger enters from the rear (right-hand edge). The dowel should be a free fit in the trigger itself, and will not be glued into the base. Make the dowel over-length, so that it can be withdrawn during the setting up and painting of the toy (see Fig. 6).

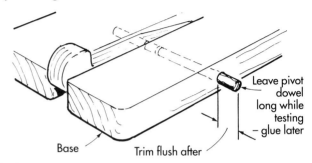

Fig. 6

4 Glue the arms to the body, noting the angle of the right one from Fig. 3. Glue the foot into the base and allow to dry.

Bend the thin piano wire ball support per the pattern, and thread the long end through the ball. Coax the bends through the holes in the ball and secure the wire with fast epoxy. The sequence is shown in Fig. 7. Form a small loop at the top to take the tiny woodscrew. You will pivot it on this screw, to the right-hand side of the right wrist after painting.

Fig. 7

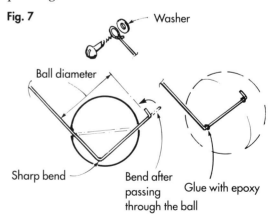

5 Finish and paint the toy parts, remove the trigger but do not fit the ball wire or the left leg and wire yet.

6 Complete the assembly, using the No.10 screw to pivot the leg when the wire is in place. Insert the other end of the wire into the trigger and push the pivot dowel through. Do not cut the excess off yet; you may have to undo it for final adjustment, or for clearing excess paint away.

   Bend the ball wire gently until the ball clears the head, and lodges against the bottom. At rest, it should hang clear of the ground and be just in line with the boot as it is struck. Do not worry that the ball and boot do not follow the same path. Your soccer player would have to have very long legs for this to happen! Have some practice thumps on the trigger to get it right before you lock the screws with epoxy, and trim that dowel flush.

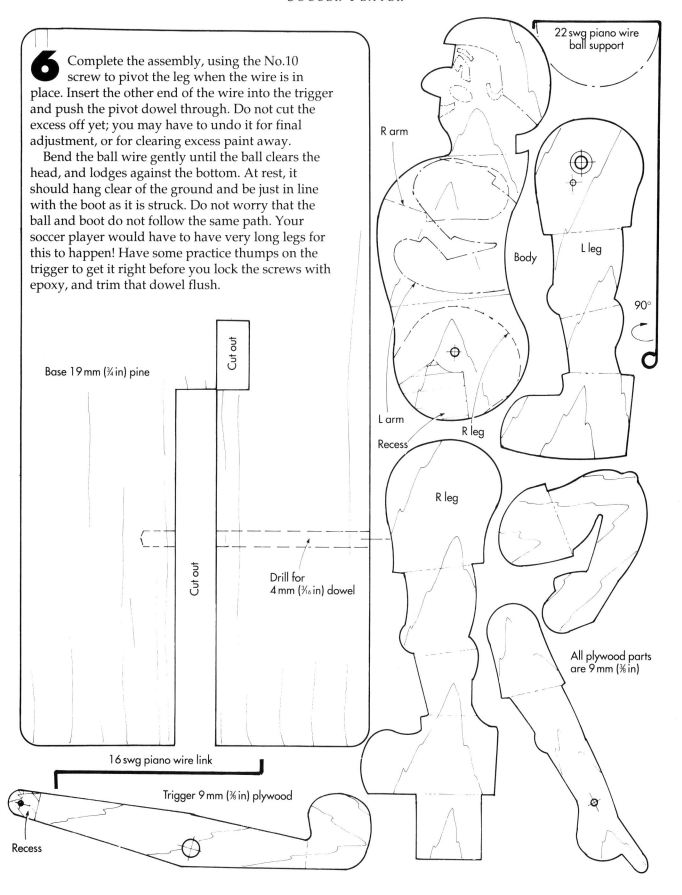

22 swg piano wire ball support

R arm

Body

L leg

90°

L arm

R leg

Recess

R leg

Base 19 mm (¾ in) pine

Cut out

Cut out

Drill for 4 mm (³⁄₁₆ in) dowel

All plywood parts are 9 mm (⅜ in)

16 swg piano wire link

Trigger 9 mm (⅜ in) plywood

Recess

HELICOPTER

This chunky little helicopter can be pulled or pushed. The rotor spins via a friction drive from the main axle and the rear wheel is disguised as a tail rotor. Cast your mind back to the Waltzers: the drive is similar and is shown in Fig. 1. Two sections are shown in Fig.2. Note that the main axle is held in place by a removable bottom. This is necessary, in order to assemble the rotor shaft and its drive disc. The fuselage is made from three laminations of pine and the bottom piece screwed on to them; then all the corners are rounded off to a more streamlined shape. Two plywood bearings support the rotor shaft, so that there is little friction. Were the shaft to run in a long hole in the fuselage, it would rub over a large area – the plywood bearings reduce the area of contact.

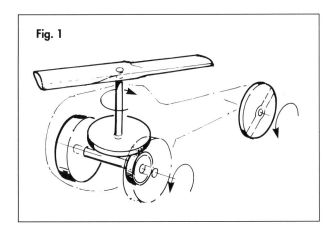

Fig. 1

MATERIALS

3 mm (⅛ in) plywood: 51 x 24 mm
(2 x 1 in)
6 mm (¼ in) plywood:
152 x 64 mm (6 x 2½ in)
19 x 9 mm (¾ x ⅜ in) pine:
223 mm (8¾ in)
120 x 19 mm (4¾ x ¾ in) pine:
559 mm (22 in)
65 x 16 mm (2½ x ⅝ in) pine:
127 mm (5 in)
6 mm (¼ in) dowel: 254 mm
(10 in)
6 x 6 mm (¼ x ¼ in) pine: 51 mm
(2 in)
One 6 x 25 mm (¼ x 1 in) rubber
band
Four No. 8 countersunk 32 mm
(1¼ in) woodscrews
PVA glue
Fast epoxy glue
Paint

TOOLS

Fretsaw
Tenon-saw
Drill
Hole saw
Chisel
Screwdriver
Rat-tail file
Paintbrushes
Sandpaper
Pencil
Carbon paper
Rule

Fig. 2

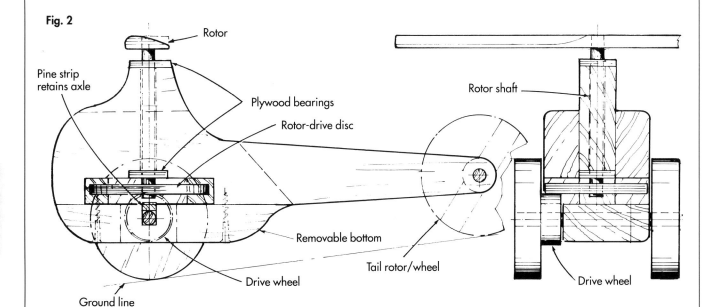

Pine strip
retains axle

Rotor

Plywood bearings

Rotor-drive disc

Rotor shaft

Removable bottom

Tail rotor/wheel

Drive wheel

Drive wheel

Ground line

1 Referring to pattern pages 107–8, drill and cut out the shaft bearings from the 3 mm (⅛ in) plywood. Use these first to check the recess in the centre fuselage lamination, after tracing its shape to the 19 mm (¾ in) pine, but before cutting it out on the fretsaw.

Now, use the bearings to centre a 6 mm (¼ in) drill for the starting hole for the shaft in the centre lamination. Keep the drill vertical while holding the

job in the vice. Open the hole out to the next drill size for good clearance, then glue the bearings top and bottom. Check that a piece of 6 mm (¼ in) dowel spins freely before allowing the bearings to set. Adjust their position until this is so. The bottom bearing should be flush each side, when the hole is central. It will then sit between the outer laminations, which you now trace down and cut out on the fretsaw.

2 Use the tenon-saw to make two diagonal cuts in each side piece, as shown on the pattern. Remove the wood in between with a chisel, to form clearance recesses for the rotor-drive disc. Drill 6 mm (¼ in) clearance at the tail end and pilot drill 1.5 mm (⅟₁₆ in) for the screws that will hold the bottom piece in place. By now, the side laminations should look like Fig. 3 when glued in place – the bearings have been shown separately for clarity.

Fig. 3

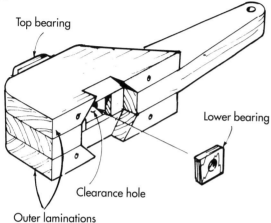

Top bearing

Lower bearing

Clearance hole

Outer laminations

3 Mark out, drill and cut the bottom fuselage piece. Chamfer the rear edge and round the front. Recess the left side to clear the drive wheel that will go on one main wheel and, using the tenon-saw, form a clearance groove for the axle. This will be just over 12 mm (½ in) deep. Lay a piece of dowel in the groove, then glue in the 6 mm (¼ in) square pine strip to the wood above the axle. Pull the dowel out and you have a bearing for the main wheels. Fig. 4 shows this stage.

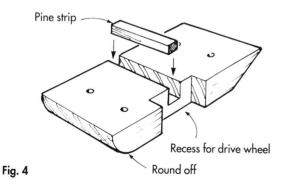

Pine strip

Recess for drive wheel

Fig. 4 Round off

4 Using the hole saw, cut out the main wheels, the rotor-drive disc and the tail wheel. Set it smaller and cut the drive wheel and tail wheel retainer. Or if your hole saw does not go this small, cut them on the fretsaw.

Cut the rotor shaft from the 6 mm (¼ in) dowel and glue it into the rotor-drive disc. It has to be truly upright, so use a pair of 90-degree cardboard templates set at right angles to each other (as in Fig. 5), to hold it there while the glue sets. Test spin the shaft before the glue is hard, to make sure that the disc does not wobble. Insert the shaft into its bearings in the fuselage from below. Test spin it again to check that it clears the recess and does not bind in the hole. If the hole needs clearing, use a small rat-tail file from both ends, but be careful that you do not make the bearings sloppy. Rub the shaft and bearings with a graphite pencil to lubricate them.

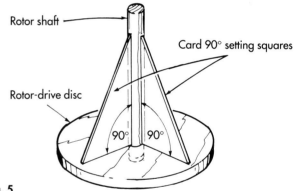

Rotor shaft

Card 90° setting squares

Rotor-drive disc

90° 90°

Fig. 5

5 Glue the drive wheel to one main wheel and add the shaft. Use fast epoxy to secure the rubber band on the drive wheel, to provide friction (as shown in Fig. 6). Keep the glue off the outside of the band and do not paint over it.

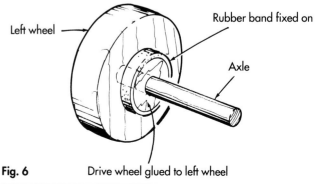

Left wheel

Rubber band fixed on

Axle

Drive wheel glued to left wheel

Fig. 6

You can now slide the axle through the slot in the lower fuselage and screw it temporarily in place. The rotor shaft should turn as the wheel is turned. It may be a little intermittent at this stage, as there is no rotor on top to press it down on to the drive. Press lightly with your finger in the top of the shaft to rectify this.

6 Cut a short piece of dowel and glue it in the tail wheel. Use the card templates to get it wobble-free. Add a small washer and pass the dowel through the fuselage boom from the right-hand side (Fig. 7). Press on the retainer and test spin for freedom. Do not glue on yet.

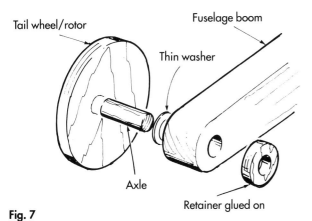

Fig. 7

Tail wheel/rotor
Fuselage boom
Thin washer
Axle
Retainer glued on

7 Take the remaining piece of 19 x 9 mm (¾ x ⅜ in) pine and drill it 6 mm (¼ in) in the centre; mark a line each side per the pattern, to guide the carving. This is a propeller shape; in other words, opposite edges are carved. Use a chisel and sandpaper to form a tapered, rounded section on top and quite flat underneath. See Fig. 8. Do not work it too thin: it has to have some weight, as explained earlier, and it needs strength.

Fig. 8

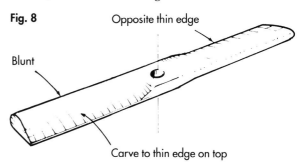

Opposite thin edge
Blunt
Carve to thin edge on top

8 Put the rotor and other wheel on dry. Test for free action, then take it apart by removing wheels, rotor and bottom piece. Finish and paint the individual components, keeping the paint off all rubbing surfaces.

When you paint the cabin windows, use mid-blue; then, when dry, take a little white paint on an almost dry brush and streak them diagonally to represent a glass-like shine. Now, paint the black cheat lines to cover any over-run of the last exercise.

TIP

Rounding dowels

Some dowels are not truly round when bought, perhaps because the machine that produced them was slightly out of adjustment. The result is often an oversize dowel or one with a ridge along it. Neither will do for axles; they will bind, or if the hole is opened out, they will be sloppy when the offending part wears down to a better shape. The diagram shows a simple sizing tool for correcting the dowel.

Use a good-quality wood clothes-peg and, if necessary, re-shape the jaws with a rat-tail file. Allow space for a piece of glasspaper, which will need frequent replacement if there is much correcting to be done. The pressure is exerted by the spring in the peg, so hold it by the sides as you rotate it and slide it along. You set the final diameter by adjusting the small woodscrew in the opposite end of the peg. This acts as a limit stop when the right size is reached.

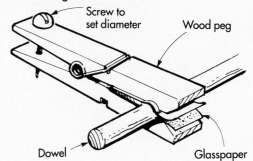

Screw to set diameter
Wood peg
Dowel
Glasspaper

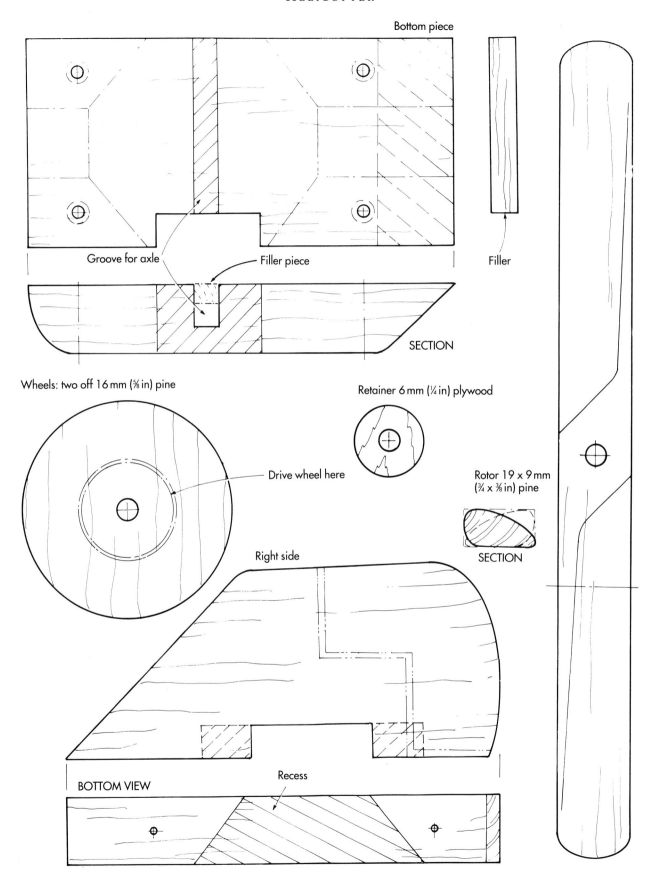

Bottom piece

Filler

Groove for axle

Filler piece

SECTION

Wheels: two off 16 mm (⅝ in) pine

Retainer 6 mm (¼ in) plywood

Drive wheel here

Rotor 19 x 9 mm
(¾ x ⅜ in) pine

SECTION

Right side

BOTTOM VIEW

Recess

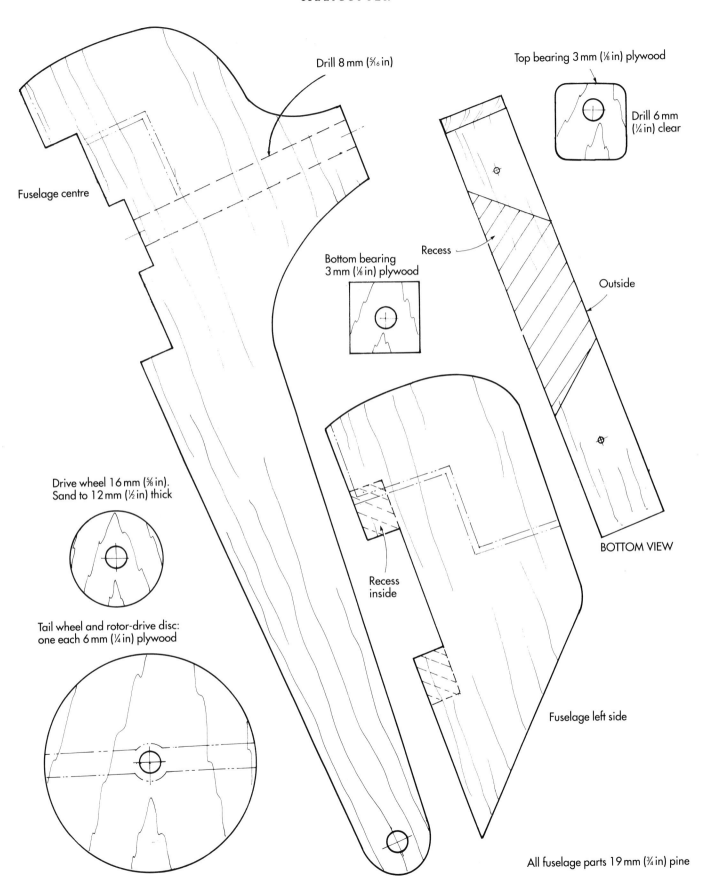

Drill 8 mm (⁵⁄₁₆ in)

Top bearing 3 mm (⅛ in) plywood

Drill 6 mm (¼ in) clear

Fuselage centre

Bottom bearing 3 mm (⅛ in) plywood

Recess

Outside

Drive wheel 16 mm (⅝ in). Sand to 12 mm (½ in) thick

Tail wheel and rotor-drive disc: one each 6 mm (¼ in) plywood

Recess inside

BOTTOM VIEW

Fuselage left side

All fuselage parts 19 mm (¾ in) pine

BUCKING BRONCO

Will the cowboy stay on the frantic fretwork foal? This pull-along toy is more than a traditional, eccentric wheeled horse. If the bucking bronco is to kick properly, the wheels providing the action have to be so large that they would hide the rear legs; small wheels merely give a fast nod to the horse. This toy solves the problem by having the horse on a steady platform and an eccentric to drive the action, from large rear wheels that are clear of the legs. Fig. 1 shows how it works. The cowboy is freely pivoted and has heavy legs, so that he does not topple over.

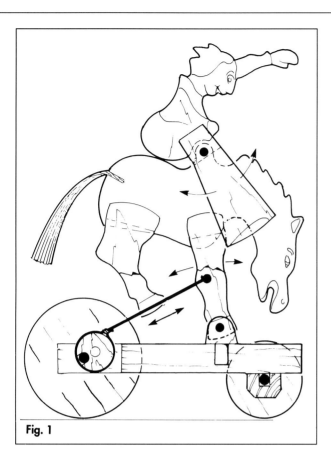

Fig. 1

1 Trace down the shapes of the base and wheels on to the 19 mm (¾ in) thick pine, from the patterns on pages 112–13. Use the hole saw to cut the small wheels and eccentric from the 9 mm (⅜ in) plywood. There will be a central hole in the latter. No matter, it does not affect the performance. Just cut the edge notch with a fretsaw. The large wheels have to be fretsawn. There is a tip to help you here on page 33.

Separate the base from the rest of the board with the tenon-saw. Cut two slits as shown and remove the intervening wood with drill and chisel – as in Fig. 2.

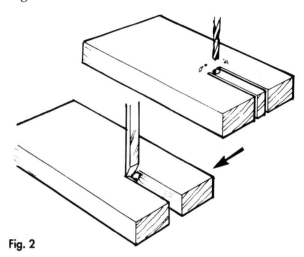

Fig. 2

2 Mark the positions of the axle hole on both edges of the base and very carefully drill from each side, to meet in the slot you made earlier. If you have a drill stand for the electric drill, use it; but you must ensure that the base is vertically on edge. Clamp a square piece of wood to it so that it stays parallel to the drill (as shown in Fig. 3).

MATERIALS

3 mm (⅛ in) plywood:
    228 x 178 mm (9 x 7 in)
9 mm (⅜ in) plywood:
    101 x 76 mm (4 x 3 in)
76 x 19 mm (3 x ¾ in) pine:
    406 mm (16 in)
19 x 19 mm (¾ x ¾ in) pine:
    76 mm (3 in)
5 mm (³⁄₁₆ in) dowel: 51 mm (2 in)
6 mm (¼ in) dowel: 241 mm
    (9½ in)
1.5 mm (¹⁄₁₆ in) steel wire:
    178 mm (7 in)
Flower wire
One No. 4 countersunk 9 mm
    (¾ in) woodscrew
Small screw eye
White string
Two thin 6 mm (¼ in) washers
PVA glue
Fast epoxy glue
Paint

TOOLS

Fretsaw
Tenon-saw
Drill
Hole saw
Chisel
Mouse-tail file
Snipe-nose pliers
Sandpaper
Pencil
Carbon paper
Paintbrushes

Fig. 3

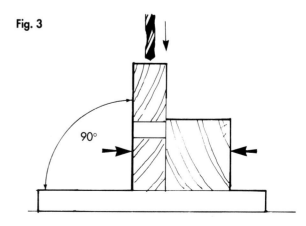

90°

3 Trace down the shapes of the horse and the cowboy's body on to the 3 mm (⅛ in) plywood. This thin material has been selected to reduce the weight of the moving parts.

Do not forget to mark the positions of the horse's legs on both sides of the body. If they are in the wrong place, it will not balance properly. The legs are splayed out, the rear ones more than the front pair. Shave a chamfer on the inner faces of each with a chisel held flat, over the hatched areas shown on the template page. Check the angles of chamfer from the full-size front views of the legs in Fig. 4.

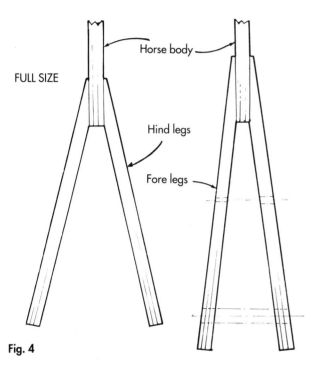

FULL SIZE

Horse body

Hind legs

Fore legs

Fig. 4

4 Before you cut out the horse's body, drill the pivot hole for the cowboy. It is near the edge, so the drill might cause it to split if the edge were cut first. You can strengthen the wood around the hole with a smear of fast epoxy glue – do not clog the hole in the process. Cut out the cowboy's body.

Cut his legs from the 9 mm (⅜ in) plywood and chamfer these too, so that they appear as in Fig. 5. Drill from the chamfered surface, so that a pivot dowel will go through in a straight line. Glue the legs to the body, using the 5 mm (³⁄₁₆ in) dowel to align them. Check that when the cowboy is on the horse, the legs prevent his body hitting the back or neck of the horse when it is tilted forward about 15 degrees. The legs act as a pendulum.

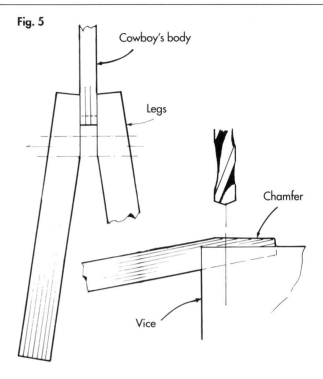

Fig. 5

Cowboy's body

Legs

Chamfer

Vice

5 Make the horse pivot from the remaining 9 mm (⅜ in) plywood, using the fretsaw, after drilling. Carve the lug below to a circular section to fit into the hole in the base, and glue it in.

6 Cut a groove with the tenon-saw in the 19 x 19 mm (¾ x ¾ in) pine strip. This forms a housing for the front axle. Shave the lower corners off with the chisel, to neaten it (as in Fig. 6). Glue it under the base as shown on the pattern page.

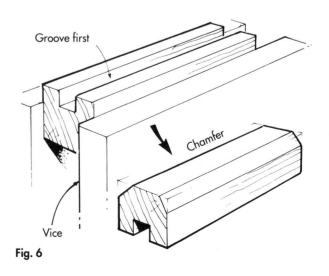

Groove first

Chamfer

Vice

Fig. 6

7 Using a mouse-tail file, form a shallow groove all round the eccentric (as shown in Fig. 7). Bend the 1.5 mm (1/16 in) wire round the groove and check the final shape on the pattern page. The wire will spring open slightly. Form the small loop to take the woodscrew that will pass through the front legs later.

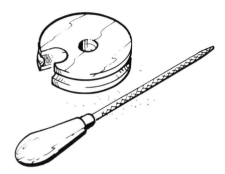

Fig. 7

8 Finish and paint all the parts before assembly, so that you can get the brush into the confined spaces. Keep the paint off the axles and pivots. When dry, re-assemble up to the point of finishing the eccentric and link.

9 Glue on one rear wheel, slide the axle through the base, then glue the eccentric via its notch on to the centre of the axle with fast epoxy. Keep the glue away from the base, so that you can still turn it afterwards! Glue on the other rear wheel.

10 Slip the eccentric wire down at the side of the eccentric in the slot (Fig. 8). Spring it over the eccentric into the groove. Bind the loose end with thin flower wire and, after checking that the eccentric turns easily, lock the thin wire with a

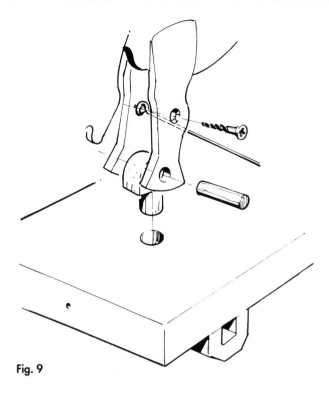

Fig. 9

spot of fast epoxy. Drive the screw through the front legs, capturing the small loop of the link wire (Fig. 9).

11 Pass the dowel pivots through and glue them at their outside ends only. Push the front axle through and glue on the front wheels.

12 Form a bunch of white string to represent a tail and glue it into the slot in the horse's rump. Unravel the strands to make it spread out.

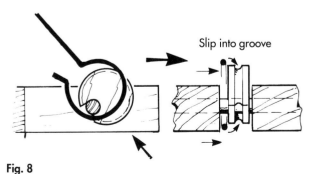

Slip into groove

Fig. 8

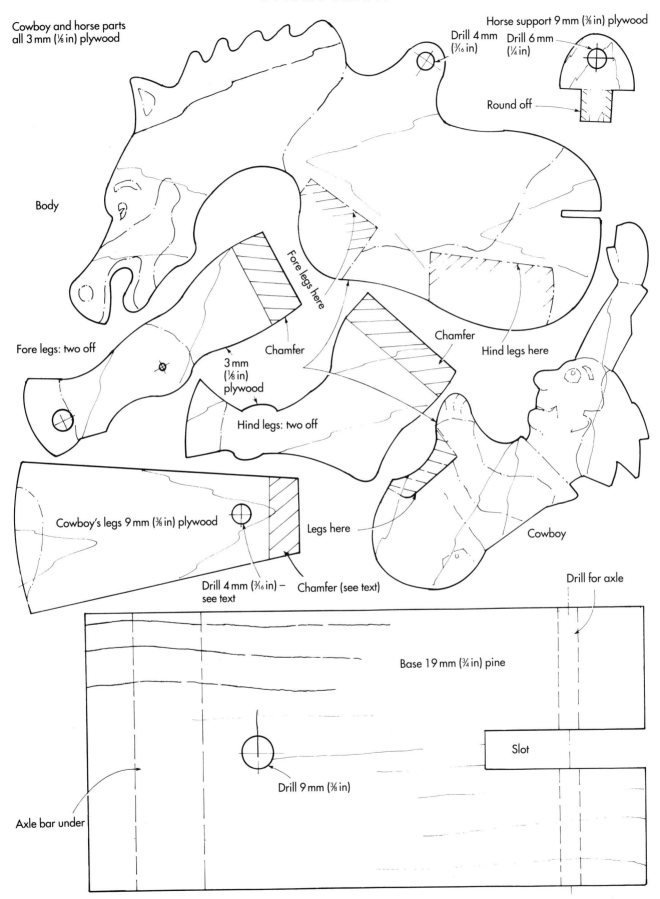

Cowboy and horse parts
all 3 mm (⅛ in) plywood

Horse support 9 mm (⅜ in) plywood

Drill 4 mm (³⁄₁₆ in) Drill 6 mm (¼ in)

Round off

Body

Fore legs here

Drill 4 mm (³⁄₁₆ in)

Fore legs: two off

3 mm (⅛ in) plywood

Chamfer

Chamfer

Hind legs here

Hind legs: two off

Cowboy

Cowboy's legs 9 mm (⅜ in) plywood

Legs here

Drill 4 mm (³⁄₁₆ in) – see text

Chamfer (see text)

Drill for axle

Base 19 mm (¾ in) pine

Slot

Drill 9 mm (⅜ in)

Axle bar under

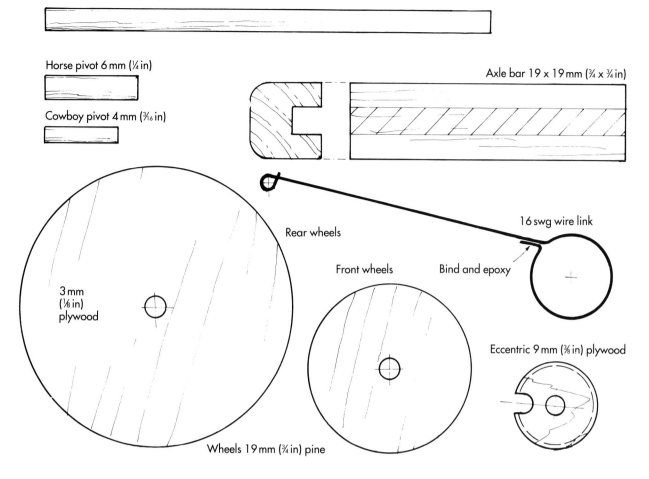

Axles: two off 6 mm (¼ in) dowel

Horse pivot 6 mm (¼ in)

Cowboy pivot 4 mm (³⁄₁₆ in)

Axle bar 19 x 19 mm (¾ x ¾ in)

16 swg wire link

Rear wheels

Front wheels

Bind and epoxy

3 mm
(⅛ in)
plywood

Eccentric 9 mm (⅜ in) plywood

Wheels 19 mm (¾ in) pine

TIP

Axle Refitting

There will be a piece of axle left in the wheel long
enough to go in the chuck of a drill. Fit the drill in its
bench stand and bring the drill down so that the wheel
sits on the drill table. Wedge it there with scraps of wood
held to the table with double-sided tape.

Loosen the drill chuck, leaving the axle and wheel
stuck down. Now slice off the axle cleanly and fit a
6 mm (¼ in) drill to the chuck. Without allowing the
wheel to move, drill out the broken axle stump. Do the
same with the other wheel; then make a new axle. This
method helps to keep the drill in the centre of the wheel,
instead of being deflected by the hardened glue.

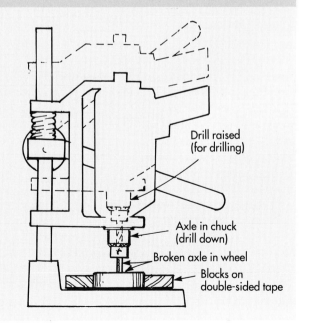

Drill raised
(for drilling)

Axle in chuck
(drill down)

Broken axle in wheel

Blocks on
double-sided tape

PAINTING

In this age of brightly coloured toys, the really traditional stained and varnished wood finish fades in the child's range of popularity. Craftsmanship is rather lost in the brash colours of mass-produced, often short-lived, items of our throw-away society.

A colourful paint finish is not a layer to cover up the work you have done: it is part of the whole subject. It attracts immediately. It protects the wood. It adds realism where required. It augments the shaping you have done on the basic material.

But how?

Sadly, paint is sometimes applied as a quick lick of colour straight over the wood, just after it looks smooth. This does not do justice to the woodwork. Why? Because, in a number of cases, the person holding the paintbrush is only thinking of the finishing colours. Finishing can take as long as the whole woodwork stage, because there is more to painting than applying paint. All too often, the result of hastily applied paint is a rippled surface, with every little part of the wood grain showing as bumps and hollows; the different colours overlapping, leave a ridge or step in the surface; and where paint has been pushed into corners, there will be shrinkage later, to expose a groove where there was initially a smooth angle.

Faced with this result some months later, the holder of the paintbrush tries to compensate on the next exercise, by sloshing on a good thick covering. This will cover the grain, but the wretched stuff pokes out at the edges, and the hollows become squishy pools that dissolve into subsequent colours. This will somewhat blur the overall effect, and small hands will receive an extra something to the blend of coal dust, mud and jam . . . so will the toy, in return, because it will be more difficult to wipe clean.

1 All the surfaces that are to be painted must be sanded until there are no whiskers, or grain texture. Pay particular attention to the edges of plywood and end-grain, and countersunk hole edges (Fig. 1).

Most toys can be painted in component parts, so that you can reach into corners and avoid getting different colours splashed on to adjacent parts. The

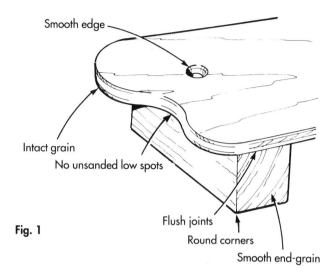

Smooth edge

Intact grain

No unsanded low spots

Fig. 1

Flush joints

Round corners

Smooth end-grain

wheels need to have the axle hole finished neatly, so that there is a minimum of smoothing during the paint stages.

Whenever possible, glue one, if not both, wheels on to their axle and sand the axle flush, or fill it flush. Fit one wheel per axle if the axle goes through a hole in the base. You can glue on both wheels if the axle will be supported in a grooved strip of wood, that will be glued on later (see Fig. 2).

Sand with progressively finer grades of abrasive paper until a silky surface is achieved. But it is not ready yet.

2 Dampen the surface of the wood with a moist cloth. Do *not* dunk it in water. Let the wood dry, allowing the grain to rise. If you miss out this stage, the grain will rise when the paint is put on. You do not want this to happen.

Once again, sand with fine-grain abrasive paper to level off the raised grain. This is known as 'de-nibbing'. Do not forget the edges too. Dust off thoroughly. You can now apply a grain filler. Water-based ones may raise the grain again; but oil- or solvent-based ones bond the surface. The prototype toys were filled with non-toxic primer – a thin coat designed to help the undercoat to adhere properly. Let it dry in a dust-free place.

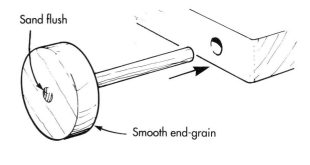

Sand flush

Smooth end-grain

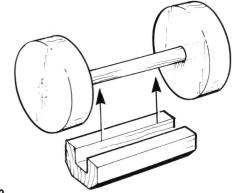

Fig. 2

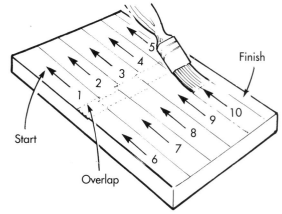

Start

Overlap

Finish

Fig. 3

3 Apply a smooth, even coat of non-toxic, oil-based white undercoat. Do not be tempted to build up a thickness in one coat. Let it dry, then give it a second, even, coat.

There is a technique for applying paint. If you have painted the house, you might have used it. However, this may be your introduction to smaller scale work, where it counts even more.

Brush the paint over to cover the job evenly. Do not dip into the paint again, but using the same brush, stroke right along the length of the work in slow, even sweeps to 'lay off' the surface more smoothly. This removes brush marks. When you have to finish a large area, start near the top. Brush upwards, then work across as before in parallel sweeps. Start again further down, and go in the same direction as the first part. Allow the brush to lift off gently as it just covers the start of the earlier sweeps. Continue in this way, never making strokes in different directions. Fig. 3 shows this technique.

Let this coat dry for about six hours, then put some 'wet and dry' fine-grade abrasive paper on the 'wet' sanding block, with a spot of washing-up liquid to lubricate it. Wet sand with enough water to wash away the paint waste.

If you go on sanding merrily, without wiping and inspecting the surface frequently, you will expose

the wood. This will make the grain rise again, which, in turn, brings you straight back to stage two!

You should be able to see when the white starts to become thin enough to be level without cutting through. If there are low spots, they will show as more shiny; you may still detect brush marks. If you can carefully get these smooth, with the paper on the tip of your fingers, you may avoid having to re-coat the area in order to fill the low spots enough. Otherwise, you may be cutting the already smooth parts too deeply.

Most of the toys have been designed so that simple flat surfaces are all that need to be tackled. The edges and sharply rounded parts are where to go gently, with fingers rather than the block. This whole sequence is shown in Fig. 4.

Fig. 4

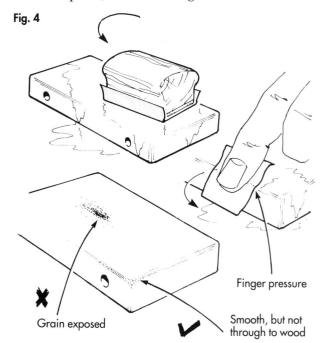

Grain exposed

Finger pressure

Smooth, but not through to wood

The undercoating and its sanding is the most important stage. If you skimp it, the high gloss of the coloured finish will show and emphasize every tiny blemish that is left.

4 The prototypes were painted with Japlac high-gloss, non-toxic lacquer, which is oil based and available in primary colours (red, blue and yellow), plus green, black and white; other shades were mixed from these. A section on colour mixing follows.

The rule of colour painting is: start with the light shades and finish with the dark; for dark will cover light more easily than vice versa.

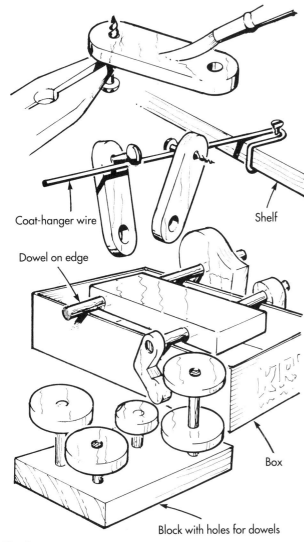

Coat-hanger wire

Dowel on edge

Shelf

Box

Block with holes for dowels

Fig. 5

Shake the paint can for several minutes to mix the heavier pigments with the lighter, oily varnish part. Use a clean stick or small spoon to put a small quantity of paint into a clean small container. The cap of a bottle, or one section of an old ice-cube tray, is ideal. You only need enough to cover the range of parts in a particular colour, or pair of toys if you are a mass-production woodworker. Left-over paint may contaminate the can stock if you return it. Tiny particles of dust may have settled in it.

Use a pair of pliers to hold parts that are mounted on scraps of dowel or on pieces of wire. This way, you can turn the part over without having to change your hold on the brush. This makes for smooth edges to each colour. Remember to use the 'lay off' technique with the colour as well; even tiny areas benefit from it. Stand each painted piece in a dust-free area to dry. You will find that old coat-hanger wires (straightened out and wedged under a shelf edge) are good hanging places for parts that are drilled. You can put a woodscrew into some holes, for you to hold it while painting, and to hook over the wire afterwards (Fig. 5). Make sure that the pieces do not touch each other.

Some of the stronger colours may need two coats, drying in between each one. Two thin coats are better than one thick one, which can form runs. Leave large, flat areas to dry in a horizontal position.

Hopefully, you will not need to wet sand the colour finish to make it smooth, because the undercoat should be perfect already, and the colour is put on evenly. If you have to smooth the colour, you will have to re-paint it to restore the even shade. If you cannot get a smooth, even colour shade with the paint straight from one can, then add a spot of white to give it extra body and opacity. In many cases, the colour looks brighter, and you should achieve a one-coat cover.

5 Paint subsequent darker areas, using artist's brushes, which are finer, so they will lay out the paint overlapping earlier areas slightly.

Blending
When you paint faces, mix a warm flesh colour to go over the white undercoat, then add a spot of red on the nose and cheeks straight on to the wet pink. Watch it spread, or blend it with a dry brush around the edge. Do not stipple hard: the pink will thin out too much. Leave dark areas and details until this stage is dry.

Lines

If you need a thin white stripe, paint the area white, let it dry, then paint colour up to the two edges with a fine brush.

I find that only larger straight edges benefit from masking off with tape. The little details can be done free-hand with a fine brush. Provided the paint underneath is dry, you can wipe off a mistake quickly with a cloth slightly moistened in white spirit; then dry it with a clean dry cloth and have a second attempt.

If you mask, use masking tape on paint that has been dry at least overnight. Press the edge down firmly with the finger, not a ruler, which might scratch the paint. Gently peel the tape right back over itself just as soon as the new paint is tack dry. If you leave it until later, there will be a ridge. If you peel it sooner, the paint may creep underneath. Straight edges can be painted quite accurately with practice. Lay a ruler along the line, tilted up so that the metal part of the paintbrush runs along it. The point of the brush is just touching the job. Use your knuckle to maintain the distance, and simply rule along smoothly. The technique is shown in Fig. 6.

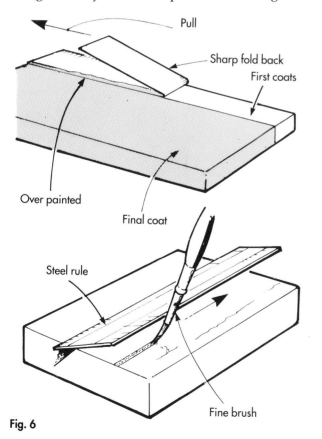

Fig. 6

Colours

The basic rules of colour mixing and their complementary colours are simple. Forget black and white for the moment; they are the absence and excess of light, but in mixing they will control the tone of the colour you choose.

There are three basic primary colours: red, blue and yellow (available in Japlac and Humbrol ranges).

As you blend pairs of primaries, you get three more colours, which are known as secondaries: for example, red and yellow, gives orange; blue and yellow, green; and blue and red, purple. Any graduation of these three mixes changes the shade towards the larger amount of each pair. Some so-called primary colours do not give a balanced mix: for example, a bright, slightly orange red does not produce a good purple with blue, but is fine for orange. A light blue does not make a strong green – rich dark blue is better with the yellow. Fig. 7 shows how the primaries combine to make secondaries.

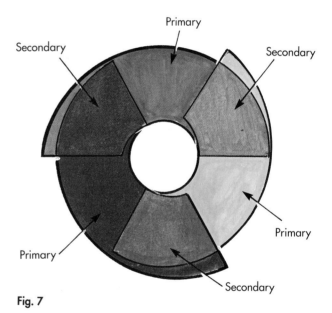

Fig. 7

Complementary colours

We see a different colour after staring very hard at one brightly lit colour. What our brain does is to reverse the colour to its opposite shade in the primary and secondary shades. Fig. 8 shows how it works.

You are left with the following: red and green, blue and orange, yellow and purple; each pair complementary to each other. These are the colours that attract most when placed close together, as in Fig. 9. Unlike the secondaries, which are a mix of adjacent primaries, the complementaries are each a diametrically opposed pair of one primary and the secondary produced by the remaining two primaries.

Opposite secondaries and primaries

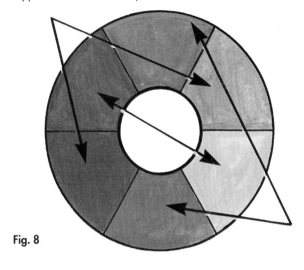

Fig. 8

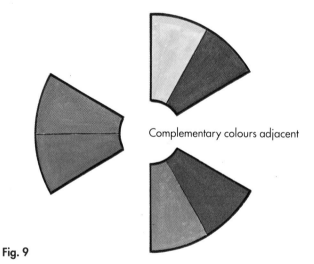

Complementary colours adjacent

Fig. 9

Dark and light

Whenever you need to darken a colour you are mixing, add a tiny spot of black to kill it a little. Always add the black in small spots, then stir before adding any more. It takes very little black to darken bright colours.

On the other hand, when you need pale colours, start by putting a little white in the mixing tray or lid, then add the primary or mixed secondary colour in small quantities. It takes a large amount of white to lighten colours, and if you start with the colours, you will finish up with more paint than you need.

Depending on the shades of your secondaries, you may have to experiment with orange and black to arrive at a suitable brown. A little blue added to the mix extends the range of brown shades.

Other mediums

Gloss enamel finishes are very hard wearing; use non-toxic, of course. However, another non-toxic finish is also suitable if you wish to try it. The finish is not so glossy, but the drying time and application may suit you better. Artist's acrylic colours obtainable at art and craft shops offer a wide range of bright colours, all of which can be diluted with water, and varnished with clear acrylic medium. If you have experience in painting with this type of paint, prepare the wood just as before, de-nibbing and sanding, but give a coat of artist's non-toxic white acrylic, and do no sanding afterwards.

If the surface is good, the matt paint finish will cover well, but there is a tendency to go too thinly, and make the result look like a delicate watercolour. This is fine and subtle for faces, but you need to 'lay off' carefully thicker, strong colours to give the toy some impact. You can also take a drawing pen with Indian ink to add details before varnishing with clear acrylic to seal it. This type of finish will not stay so clean, and it may scuff off when used outdoors.

SHARPENING TOOLS

Chisels will need the most attention while making these projects. A keen edge will ensure accurate work. A blunt chisel can refuse to go where you direct it. Use one and you will cut yourself, and be disappointed with the surface that you are trying to shape. If the grain is not straight or you are cutting diagonally, a blunt chisel will be deflected by the fibres along the wrong line, instead of slicing through them.

When you buy a new chisel, it will probably be ground to the right clearance angle, but it may need a final honing to finish and polish the actual cutting edge. Yes, it will cut, but just compare the difference when you have given it that final treatment. It will slide like silk, leave a really smooth surface and take hardly any effort to push with the hand. You can then devote more of your energy to coaxing it to follow the intended line, rather than fighting with the wood.

Fig. 1 shows the 20-degree grinding angle that is the basis of the chisel shape when bought. The side bevels, also shown, have nothing to do with the cutting: they enable you to cut into restricted corners.

Sharpening applies to the extreme tip of the ground edge (as in Fig. 2). It will be 25 degrees for normal work or a little more steep for really hard hardwoods. You can use a carborundum sharpening stone lubricated with oil. It has a coarse and a fine side for finishing. More recently, woodworkers have found the Chinese water stones give a better, cleaner result.

The stone must be quite flat. Lay the cutting face of the chisel on the stone. Tilt the blade up 25 degrees and draw it back towards you in an S-shaped path covering most of the stone surface, with gentle pressure. Return, completing a figure eight without pressure (as in Fig. 3). Keep checking that you are doing it evenly. More pressure on one side will result in a rounded or splayed end (as in Fig. 4). After a while, you will feel or see a tiny lip on the flat side (back) of the tip. This is called a burr. The metal has become so thin that it has bent. It shows that the tip has been formed. Turn the chisel flat on its back on the stone and draw it back away from the tip, until pieces of the burr fall off. Hold it up to the light. If you can see light reflected on the actual

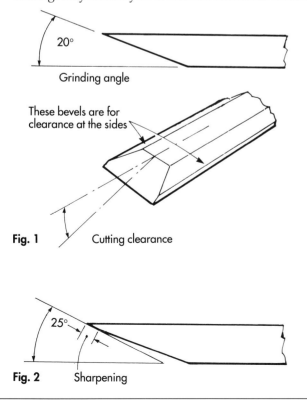

Fig. 1

20°
Grinding angle

These bevels are for clearance at the sides

Cutting clearance

25°
Fig. 2 Sharpening

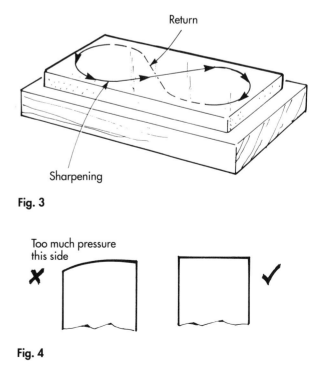

Return

Sharpening

Fig. 3

Too much pressure this side

Fig. 4

edge, it needs a few more strokes on the face and another on the back. It may feel and look sharp, but there is more to do. First, clean any metal particles from the stone. Now for the polish.

Take a flat piece of leather to form a strop, and put a little honing compound on it. This will complete the job and polish the cutting area so that it slides through the wood more easily. Stroke the chisel back away from the edge five times at 25 degrees on the face, then once flat on the back. Do this sequence several times. In the course of working, return to the strop occasionally for a few sequences to maintain the edge. In this way, it will be some time before you have to resort to the stone.

WORKSHOP SAFETY

1 When you finish using a tool, put it in its rack. If chisels are left in the shavings on the bench, you may brush against the edge in tidying up, or looking for a small component.

2 Wear a breathing mask when dry sanding, or using a power tool that throws out dust. Wear one when sweeping the floor too. A vacuum cleaner is a better tool for the floor.

3 Mind your knuckles when using a belt sander. Never feed small pieces of wood against the direction of the belt. They will fly back at you.

4 Always clamp the wood when using a tool with both hands. If the tool needs both hands, your left foot is not the right type of clamp!

5 If you use a tool that can be held in one hand, keep the other out of its path when holding wood down.

6 Do not peer closely over the top of a working power fretsaw. Some do not have a safety guard, and a broken piece of blade or its carrier can fly up into your face. Goggles should be worn, even over your glasses.

7 If someone speaks to you while you are using a power tool, ignore them. They should know better. Switch off before you take your eyes off the job.

8 Keep cables away from the work area; plug below bench level and unplug if the tool has a lock-on button. Check this type before plugging in or switching on the workshop supply. If one is locked on and plugged in with the supply off, all hell will break loose when the power is restored!

9 When wet sanding, keep the water away from plugs and sockets and electric tools.

Choosing Wood

The wood that you will need for the projects can be bought at a local yard or at DIY centres catering for the carpentry aspect of the hobby. You will find that planed wood saves you time and energy, and it is slightly smaller than the sawn sections from which is machined. You will be looking for pine which, along with spruce, is a common softwood that is easily worked. The plywood that is used for other parts of the toys should be just as easily obtained, but the very thinnest may be found in model shops – otherwise subsitute thin plastic laminate.

From the log
Thin and narrow boards may be cut by the wood-yard from larger ones. Just where in the log they started will determine how they will behave later (as Fig. 1 shows).

Knots will make shaping difficult and the grain, waving around them, will deflect the chisel and even make sanding more tricky. Fig. 2 shows three defects associated with poor wood. When a defect occurs in a small strip section, the wood will warp badly and probably break where the grain is sharply angled (as in Fig. 3).

Dowels
It is most important that dowels, which are used for axles, have really straight grain and are initially straight and, of course, are perfectly round in

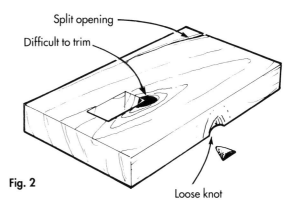

Split opening

Difficult to trim

Loose knot

Fig. 2

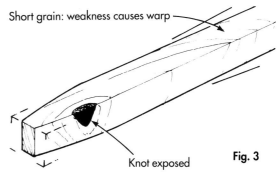

Short grain: weakness causes warp

Knot exposed   **Fig. 3**

section. Fig. 4 explains by comparison. The lower example will not only warp and break, but it will not run easily in a round hole. Slight warps may not show up on a short length that is used for an axle, but if you let it roll down a sloping board, you will detect a jerky movement at lower angles of tilt (see Fig. 5 overleaf).

Fig. 4

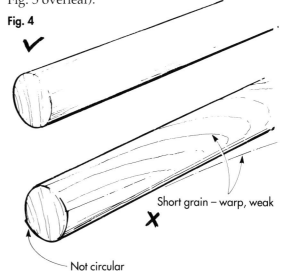

Short grain – warp, weak

Not circular

Fig. 1

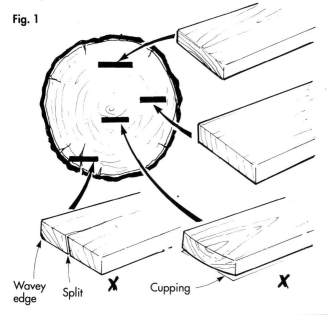

Wavey edge   Split   **X**   Cupping   **X**

Plywood
Thin 'three ply' may be light in colour; the better being birch, which is close grained, smooth and

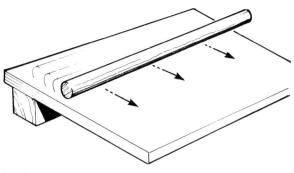

Fig. 5

strong. The laminations are usually of equal thickness, making it bend more across than along the outer grain (Fig. 6). By contrast, some mahogany ply sold as waterproof can have a thick centre and thin outer laminations. The grain is more open and a little softer. You need to sand and fill this more (Fig. 7). Multi-ply is thick, strong and heavier. It has five,

Fig. 6

Stiff

Small

Large

Fig. 7

Open grain

Thin outer

Thick centre

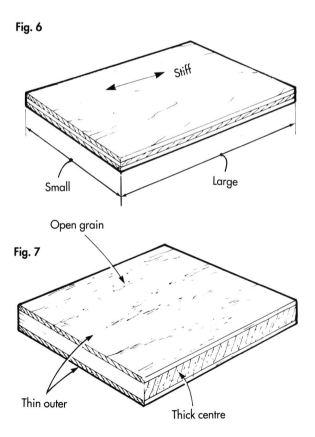

seven or more laminations and it is light coloured and smooth. It is really good for parts that are to take wear and tear (see Fig. 8).

By contrast, avoid the example in Fig. 9. This is a cheap plywood, used for backing and packing. Between the outer laminations there may be a layer with large knots, splits and gaps. This will break and leave holes where you cut across one of these hidden

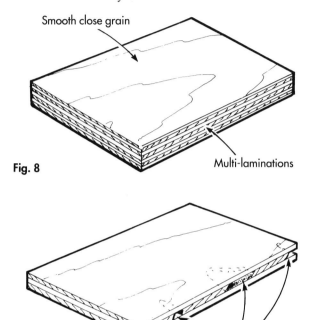

Smooth close grain

Fig. 8

Multi-laminations

Fig. 9

X

Damaged centre

blemishes. It is no good for small intricate parts. You may be able to spot an edge blemish before you commit this material to use. Look at a corner: the glue may have failed – a sure sign of low quality.

Although the amount of wood in these toys is quite small, it pays to choose carefully, rather than scratch around the oddments bin in the shed.

TOOLS IN DETAIL

The hand tools that you need for making a project are really quite limited; perhaps you already have more than enough in your household tool-box. The toys are not large jobs, compared with say, the making of a kitchen stool or mending a fence. You can, therefore, be selective and choose the better tools that can be sharpened properly for the more careful work that small items need. This is not to say that these projects involve super skilled work. You will achive much better results with the right tools, simple though they are. Each project lists the essential tools that you need to make it. A few extra ones will make things a little easier in some cases. If you were building the entire range of projects, you would not need more than the following essentials.

Marking out

For transferring the shapes from the full-size patterns that follow each constructional project, you need the following domestic items (shown in Fig. 1).

Pencil
For tracing and marking. Use an HB. Carpenter's pencils are broad and wear down more slowly. These are fine for marking the wood, but keep them to a sharp chisel point. They are no good for tracing the pattern shapes though. Use a normal pencil for this, not a ball point, as will be seen later.

Pencil Compass
A school type is suitable if strongly made. Use it to measure distances and draw wheels.

Grease-proof paper
On to which you trace the pattern shapes. Do not be tempted to use carbon paper directly under the pages in this book. It is difficult to position the wood under the book. In any case, the book will suffer in its trips to and from the work-bench! Buy the paper from stationers or the cake-making area of a food store. It is cheaper than tracing paper and almost as easily seen through, as you trace the lines.

Masking tape
Use this to hold the paper to the pattern page in the book. A tiny piece in opposite corners is enough to stop the paper slipping and changing the shape as you trace it. It peels off again without damaging the page, provided you do it slowly, unlike transparent plastic tape (Sellotape), which is fine when you want to stick paper together more firmly.

Carbon paper
When you are ready to transfer the pattern shape from the grease-proof paper to the wood, use the carbon side down on the wood and tape the tracing over it. Go over the lines with a hard (2H) pencil or a ball-point pen, which will show where you have been, as you draw over the pencil tracing you made.

Woodwork measuring and checking
The following essential items common to most projects are shown in Fig. 2.

Rule
Use a metal one with inches and millimetres. This speeds things up when reading the dimensions and checking the wood sizes. It is also hard and accurate, so that it does not flex like a retractable tape. It can be used to mark against with a knife, although a separate straight metal strip is a more professional thing for this purpose.

Try-square
A carpenter's tool for marking exact right angles and checking before and after cutting. You can also use a sliding bevel. This is adjustable for measuring angular cuts and joints. You can set it from the pattern pages. Although useful, it is not as essential as the try-square. Another type is the combination square. This can be set to right angle or 45-degree, mitre angles and it has a spirit-level and a calibrated rule that slides. It does the job of the try-square and rulers as well. Take your pick, but make sure you have a proper right-angle facility.

Marking knife
Use this to mark the wood permanently, where a cut has to be made. Do not use it where the finished surface will be incised by it.

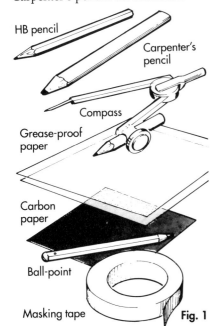

HB pencil

Carpenter's pencil

Compass

Grease-proof paper

Carbon paper

Ball-point

Masking tape

Fig. 1

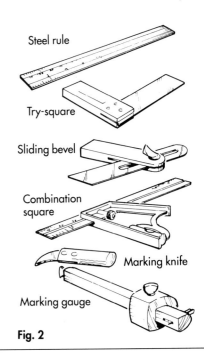

Steel rule

Try-square

Sliding bevel

Combination square

Marking knife

Marking gauge

Fig. 2

It cuts the surface grain cleanly and reduces the chances of a saw cut or chisel stroke lifting splinters on the surface.

Marking gauge
This is a block of wood which can be slid along a rod that carries a steel marking point. It scribes a line parallel to the edge of the wood along which you pull it. It too leaves a groove.

Cutting
Hand, as opposed to power, saws are shown in Fig. 3.

Handsaw
Your larger saw is probably what is known as a Combination Saw. It may have about eight teeth to the inch (3 mm apart). Use it to cut rectangles of plywood and to separate larger pieces of pine board into sizes that will be fretsawn or cut with a tenon-saw later.

Tenon-saw
This stiff-backed saw has a much finer set of teeth. Use it to make accurate straight cuts, mainly in the pine boards and strips.

Fig. 3

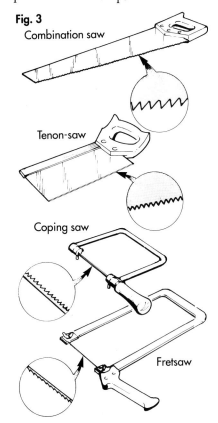

Combination saw

Tenon-saw

Coping saw

Fretsaw

Shaping
Coping saw
This is a frame-saw with a fine blade; not as fine as a hand fretsaw, but a tool for sawing out fancy shapes and taking out wood between saw cuts in forming a notch, for example. It is not absolutely vital to have one if you have a power scroll-saw. It is useful, however, because the blade can be turned sideways or forwards to get into corners.

Hand fretsaw
This is intended for light work with thin wood. If you use a thicker blade, you can, at a pinch, do all the thick cutting in pine on these toys. You need a cutting guide and clamp. It is essential that you keep the blade upright, particularly when cutting thick wood or several layers at the same time.

Power fretsaw or scroll-saw
Two different names for the same tool. Scroll-saws generally handle thicker wood, but small vibrating, short-stroke, electric fretsaws will cope (if slowly) and leave a very smooth cut edge. The two are shown in Fig. 4. The vibrating electric saw relies on a sprung frame to pull the blade up after each cutting stroke, whereas the scroll-saw or power fretsaw has a powerful return stroke and takes thicker blades, should you wish to use them.

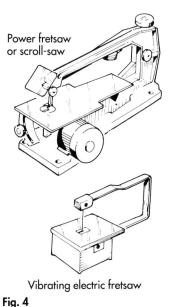

Power fretsaw or scroll-saw

Vibrating electric fretsaw

Fig. 4

Chisels
You need only a few of these – starting at 6 mm (¼ in) wide for trimming narrow slots and notches, to 25 mm (1 in) for smoothing larger areas and cutting along the grain. The bevel-edged types get into corners easily. See Fig. 5.

Holes
Awl
A small piercing tool, with a narrow chisel-edged point for marking the positions of holes and starting very small screw holes. Use it with the blade across the grain, so that it cuts, rather than forcing the grain apart and splitting it. See Fig. 6.

Fig. 5

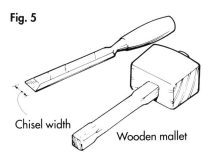

Chisel width

Wooden mallet

Fig. 6

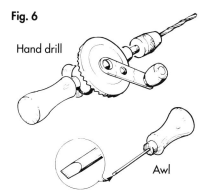

Hand drill

Awl

Hand drill
Not essential if you have an electric drill. You can get into tight corners of small jobs, though.

Electric drill
Universal tool in most people's tool-box (Fig. 7). The mains type sees more use in my workshop than the cordless type, mainly because it has the power to drive a variety of accessories (that are needed when the other is on charge). The following are used with the electric drill and are shown in Fig. 8.

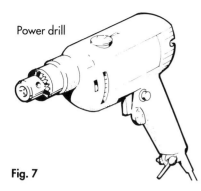

Power drill

Fig. 7

Drill stand
Essential for accuracy and control of depth. You need a very good eye to do without one.

Fig. 8

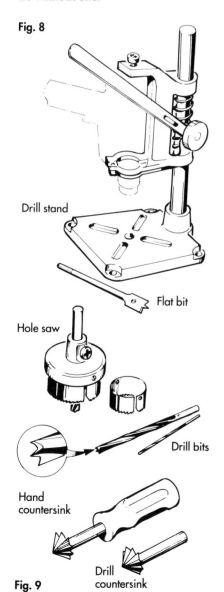

Drill stand

Flat bit

Hole saw

Drill bits

Hand countersink

Drill countersink

Fig. 9

Flat bit
Holes for the larger 12 mm (½ in) dowels in these projects are made with flat drill bits that are intended only for use in power drills. You need to use care, particularly when finishing the hole, as there is a risk of making it larger than intended.

Hole saw
This is a key tool for a number of the projects. It cuts circles in wood for use as wheels, leaving a hole in the centre that fits the dowel that will be used as an axle. It has several interchangeable cutting blades for various diameters. Use it in the power drill, preferably when in its bench stand.

Drill bits
There are special types for woodwork; the spurs shown make a cleaner hole, but you can also use the standard type if they are sharp. You will need drills from 1.5 to 7 mm (¹⁄₁₆ to ⁵⁄₁₆ in) in a set.

Countersink
This is a hand tool, for making a conical recess for screw heads, or for slightly enlarging a hole that has to be drilled again with a larger bit. It is shown in Fig. 9, with a version for hand drills, or power drills. Go easy on the latter – you can overdo it!

Rat-tail and mouse-tail files
Use these for opening out holes and forming grooves (Fig. 10).

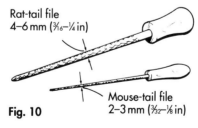

Rat-tail file
4–6 mm (³⁄₁₆–¼ in)

Mouse-tail file
2–3 mm (³⁄₃₂–⅛ in)

Fig. 10

Fixing
Screwdrivers
There never seem to be enough! You must have the right one for the screw you are driving. Fig. 11 shows what happens if they do not match.

Hammer
A small Warrington type will do for putting in panel-pins and staples. See Fig. 11.

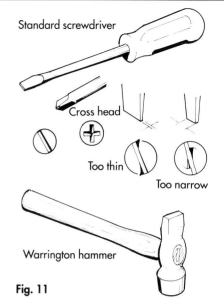

Standard screwdriver

Cross head

Too thin

Too narrow

Warrington hammer

Fig. 11

Finishing
Plane
There is not much scope for the use of a plane in these projects, that is unless you want to use wood that is not already sold as PAR (planed all round) or PSE (planed square edge). Two planes are shown in Fig. 12: a 200 mm (8 in) smoothing type is more common. You may use a plough plane for cutting narrow grooves, but few people own such a traditional piece.

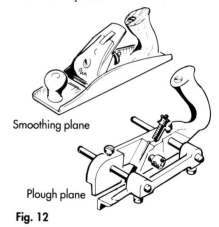

Smoothing plane

Plough plane

Fig. 12

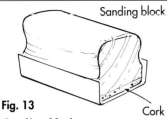

Fig. 13

Sanding block
Make this yourself as in Fig. 13, if you do not already have one. In fact, you need two, because the second one will get wet as you sand the paint finish. The belt sander has already been mentioned, but keep it dry!

Paintbrushes
You need small soft 12 and 25 mm (½ and 1 in) household types for undercoating and enamelling, then artist's No. 1 and No. 4 watercolour types for adding details and getting into corners.

Wire parts
Snipe-nose pliers
Strong box-joint type, about 75 mm (3 in) jaws with cutting edge (Fig. 14).

Soldering-iron
About 75 watt; used only for the Skater project (Fig 15).

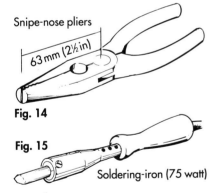

Fig. 14

Fig. 15

On the bench
Bench vice
If you have a work-bench, the vice you use should have large, wide jaws, suitable for woodwork, as in Fig. 16. A small metalwork vice will also help, although, with only wire parts to form, it may not be essential.

Portable work-bench
The folding, clamping work-bench, such as a Workmate, will serve both as bench and vice. Many households already have one in addition to, or in place of, a fixed workshop bench.

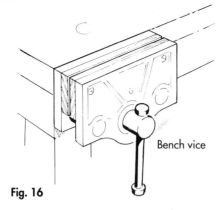

Fig. 16

Bench hook
Make this yourself according to the sizes in Fig. 17. It hooks over the bench edge or clamps in the Workmate; important when sawing accurately across the work.

Bench stop
Another to make, if the bench does not have one; useful when planing (see Fig. 18).

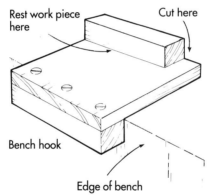

Fig. 17

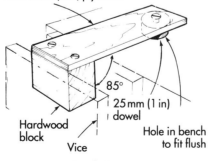

Fig. 18

Optional extras
Hand-held circular saw
This is not absolutely essential, even though many households have one (Fig. 19). You can strip large timber down to width and form a groove by setting the depth and fence accessory to suit. The wood does have to be held firmly in a vice or Workmate, and small section strips need supporting by a larger one underneath.

Router
I have not mentioned a router. It is a fine tool for many of my other woodworking applications, but the small parts used in these toys would need to be held down carefully when worked on with such a tool. I have described how to form notches, recesses and grooves by other means, and unless you already are proficient in the use of this tool, I suggest that you work mainly with hand tools as described. To buy a router *just* for the use it would get in making some features of these toys would seem wasteful.

Having read through the list, you may feel that it is a large one. Indeed, many other small woodworking jobs need more tools. Let us see what you can get away with, for the most efficient use of time and effort:

- Tracing kit (grease-proof paper, carbon paper)
- Marking kit (pencil, compass, rule, try-square)
- Power drill and stand with hole saw and two flat bits, plus normal drill bits
- Handsaw, tenon-saw, power fretsaw
- 6 mm (¼ in) chisel
- Awl, Stanley knife
- Mouse-tail and rat-tail files
- Soldering-iron
- Snipe-nose pliers
- Screwdrivers
- Small hammer
- Bench hook
- Portable work-bench
- Paintbrushes
- Sandpaper

Read through the projects, choose which you wish to make and compare the tool lists to arrive at the bare minimum, which I think most of you will have already in your tool-boxes.

Index